The Skinny Black Girl's Guide to Freedom

How to Build Unbreakable
Confidence to Master Your Life

———————————

Whitney L. Barkley, M.S.

The Skinny Black Girl's Guide to Freedom
Copyright © 2017 by Whitney L. Barkley, M.S.

Printed in USA by 48HrBooks (www.48HrBooks.com)

DEDICATION

Dear Queen:

This book is dedicated to you and the unmatched courage you have to be released from where you are to live a life of abundance that is waiting for you. No matter how dark your past or current circumstances may be, remember, self-awareness is power. Self-awareness is freedom.

Once you know who you are, nothing and no one can stop you from finding, claiming, and defining your power. Use it.

TABLE OF CONTENTS

ACKNOWLEDGMENTS

I want to thank the Academy, but I realize that it isn't my time yet. Instead, I would like to first thank God for keeping me throughout all of these years and showing me that I had a life worth living. Each day, I am learning obedience is better sacrifice, and I thank God for showing me that he is the GPS to my life. I would also like to thank my wonderful parents, Robert and Rosiemay – without them, there would be no "Skinny Black Girl." Contrary to my actions, I absorbed more from you than you'll ever know. It is a blessing and an honor to have you as parents.

Jerome, my husband, my rock, my friend – thank you for growing with me through all these years and loving me for who I am. You helped me find my strength and continue to push me to tell my story. I love and appreciate you, always and forever.

To my fellow support system of writers: Tina, Stephanie, Jacqueline, and Chalexis – thank you for your feedback and encouragement to keep pushing through with this book. I am indebted to your support and thank you for allowing me to be vulnerable and transparent with you.

To my best friends Annie and Quiarus – we've done some crazy things together. Blood couldn't make us closer and I am happy to have life-long friends who support me to the moon and back.

Damon Gilbert – my spiritual brother. Thank you for always praying with me and encouraging me to keep God first. I am so grateful for your friendship.

Last, but certainly not least, thank you to all of my supporters, readers, featured women, and podcast listeners of skinnyblackgirlscode.com. Who would ever think a blog that started off about self-esteem and image, would reach thousands of women across the world? I love you all and thank you for rockin' with me since 2014. Your support is not taken lightly. You have changed my life and are the reason that this book exists.

If I forgot anyone, please blame my mind and not my heart. I am truly thankful for everyone who has crossed my path to help me become the woman I am today. Siblings, aunts, uncles, cousins, grandparents, friends, teachers, mentors, coaches, step family, Mifflin High School family, Wilberforce family, extended family, family friends, random strangers on airplanes, etc., thank you! I believe everything happens for a reason and you all have touched a place in my heart. *Carpe Diem.*

FOREWORD

I have known Whitney Barkley for nearly five years. We met as we both were building our businesses and brands in the early stages and have grown to become business besties, accountability partners, and friends. Whitney encourages me to push my own limits, and as you read this book, she will do the same for you. Challenges happen to all of us and Whitney's "clutch-your-pearls" honesty reminds you that you are not alone in life.

Whitney is the type of woman everyone wants to be around. She is always upbeat and smiling. You would never know the hurdles of low self-esteem, colorism, bullying, and depression she's conquered based on her go-getter demeanor but nevertheless, she exemplifies the phrase "Strong Black Woman". This book is a true inspiration for any woman who questions her worthwhile secretly dealing with taboo societal issues. What you will gain from Whitney's personal journey that she realizes and exudes the power to be who you are in the face of adversity. Life choices are often personal decisions women tend to base on the approval and comfort of others. Through her courage and determination, Whitney shows us that you do not have to give up your personal freedom or sacrifice your peace to please others. Instead, as Whitney shows us, we all should focus on creating a lifestyle that holistically addresses our truths so that we gain clarity on how boldly embody the future with confidence.

Over the course of our relationship, I learned that Whitney earnestly is the real deal for bringing the best out of women. I have watched her tirelessly work with women of all ages and races to help them become the best versions of themselves and this book is another way for her to magnify the strength of a woman.

I challenge you to not let The Skinny Black Girl's Guide to Freedom be "just" another book that you purchase and read. Take time to reflect on the struggles you face or have faced in your journey to womanhood. Dig deep and pick your favorite nuggets from each chapter and apply Whitney's words of encouragement and advice to the storms that may occur in your life. Whitney has a collection of resources available to keep you energized and on the path of moving forward. Connect with her beyond these pages and do not be afraid to share your story.

Your strength is within and you can draw from Whitney's strength to keep you keep fighting for the confidence and freedom you deserve.

Jacqueline V. Twillie, MBA
Best-Selling Author of Navigating the Career Jungle
Founder of Zero Gap

Introduction

I first lost my confidence in the third grade. For eight solid years, I never had issues with my appearance. I loved the little girl that I saw in the mirror. I was smart, had a big imagination, and could care less about how my hair looked in barrettes or if I wore the latest Nikes or Air Jordans. I was perfectly happy with my eight-year-old self. As long as I had Barbies, crayons, paper, and scissors, I lived happily in my play bubble without a care in the world.

Then, came Brandon. Brandon was a fifth grader and a big bully. Each day I would briefly glance at him walk home from school poking fun at other kids or beating them up. I would walk quickly, not out of fear, but out of excitement; I had a regular play date with my dolls when I got home from school. I didn't have time to worry about a bully....until he had time to worry about me after school one day during the spring.

I remember it like yesterday. It was beginning to warm up, the snow had melted, and Brandon was harassing the usual suspects. Of course, I was in my little world, minding my business when Brandon grabbed me by my book bag and shoved me on the ground.

"You ug-lee!" He gleefully shouted as he stared at me on the ground. I laid on the hard concrete of the sidewalk for a second, partially in shock from Brandon putting his hands on me and partly embarrassed because he called me ugly. No one had ever said that word to me before. Was it true? My mind began to whirl as I started to question everything I ever felt about my appearance.

Brandon walked away from me and continued to harass other kids. He would go on to call me ugly and hit me for another few days before I told my mom. She told me what most black parents tell their kids, "If someone hits you, you hit them back." So I did. When Brandon touched me for the second week in a row, I hit him with my house key firmly squeezed in my palm. This climactic act of defiance surprised Brandon, and we got into a bloody brawl that led us both to the principal's office the next day.

Our principal, Mrs. Otterbein, told us to stay away from each other. She tried to interrogate me about Brandon, and I told her everything -- except the fact that he called me ugly. That small detail made me uneasy. I was having a hard time trying to decide if I believed it or not and was afraid that if I said it out loud, Mrs. Otterbein might have affirmed Brandon's statement.

After being in the hot seat, Brandon reluctantly stopped targeting me on our way home from school, and I didn't have to fight back. While the bullying stopped for the year, his words continued to echo through my mind. Before I was carefree and unbothered by what the world thought; however, with the utterance of two words with powerful three syllables, the confidence I once had in myself was shattered. While Brandon's words didn't stop me from moving forward and living life, as usual, I look back and realize at that moment, the 100% confident Whitney as I knew her, no longer existed.

Getting Back You (1.0)

The moment you allow the opinions of others dictate how you feel about yourself is the moment you stop knowing who you are.

Fortunately, for many of us, this realization is lost at a young age. In the seventeenth century, an English philosopher named John Locke theorized the term, "tabula rasa" which represents the mind in its pure and primitive state. Locke believed that each one of us is born with a "blank slate, " and our identity is largely defined by experiences and life events that influence how we view the world and ourselves.

You see, when we are born, it's almost ascertained that while we may be born with only our most natural instincts of survival, we are born fearless. Babies know no limits. They do not understand the dangers of the world, have no concept of beauty, are not self-proclaimed Democrats or Republicans, are unsure about the color of their skin and how it dictates their place in society, and have not yet experienced feelings of embarrassment or disappointment.

Babies merely exist – but with admirable qualities.

Because of what they do not know, they develop in the early stages without self-imposed fears or influence from the world around them until they are about 18 months old. Erik Erikson, a child psychologist suggests, during that stage, they become introduced to the abstract emotions of shame and doubt, because they are growing into their independence and developing their abilities. Depending on the child, she may or may not receive adequate encouragement in her environment to help her succeed.

This critical stage is the prelude to emotions that many of us face today: fear, uncertainty, doubt, shame, anxiety, and others. While it is easy to argue that these feelings are a regular part of life, it is still pretty hard not to be envious of the day-old version of yourself. You 1.0 may not know what you know now, but you possessed a boldness that did not yet have an imprint by your parents, siblings, strangers, friends, teachers, bullies, employers, and other players in the world. You began life with a clean slate that allowed you to have confidence that you did not yet know that you had. The negative feelings I mentioned earlier, whether they are self-inflicted or externally imposed by your environment, hold your freedom hostage, every time they emerge or reoccur in your life. With those emotions, your clean slate is written, and the perspective you have about yourself becomes clouded.

Chances are, you picked up this book because you may be looking for a version of the clean slate you once had. Somewhere down the line, you stopped being you and may be chasing the notion that you need to find yourself, stat. I want to be the first person to tell you that you never "lost yourself"; you just forgot who you are. Each experience that we go through in life may make us more knowledgeable, but consider (negative) experience as a distraction. They become distractions because we often do one of two things: 1) We dwell on negative experiences for so long that we do not allow ourselves room to manifest in new experiences 2) We do not address our emotions and try to bury them. As a result, we act out of our character or have abrupt and sporadic changes in our behavior because we have unfinished business within ourselves.

What is Personal Freedom?

Throughout this guide, I invite you into parts of my life that I never thought I would re-explore. For the sake of this book, that exploration was necessary because you can't write a self-help book with freedom in the title and still hold on to unchecked baggage. Many of the stories that I share will be little dark, and if you know me personally or follow me on my online platform The Skinny Black Girl's Code, you may be shocked by the things that I have been through to get to a place of personal freedom today.

Freedom. This word carries so much weight but varies in definition based on the person who defines it. For me, freedom is being able to look in the mirror and be more than okay with the woman I see looking back at me physically, mentally, emotionally, and spiritually. I wholeheartedly believe that once you accept and celebrate who you are, you become impenetrable. You are cognizant that negative emotions may temporarily consume you, but they do not dictate where you are going in your life. No one or nothing can break your confidence because you know that a healthy level of self-awareness allows you to be limitless in all you do.

It took me years to define what freedom meant to me because I did not realize that I was captive to a past that was holding me back from realizing my full potential. In the coming chapters, you will learn how to define what freedom means to you and learn the steps I took to find and maintain it.

How to Use This Book

I am a little different, so naturally, I wrote a book that is equivocally yoked. Each chapter contains a combination of personal stories, research, reflections, and exercises to help guide your journey to freedom. While you can skip to the sections that sound most relevant to you, I recommend reading this book from front to back so you can get a full understand of the stories told. Many of stories are intertwined and contain important details to consider in subsequent chapters. Here's a quick summary of what to expect:

Chapter One: Layaway Life
Explains why you leave your freedom in the layaway every time you allow your past or negative emotions consume you.

Chapter Two: Forgiveness is Freedom
Contains a central theme about the importance of forgiveness for yourself and others to truly have the freedom you desire.

Chapter Three: My Size Does Not Define My Worth
Dives deep into body image as told by "The Skinny Black Girl." Provides tips and exercises to help you embrace your body and feel good about what you see.

Chapter Four: Worthy As F***
Your past does not define your present or future. You are not what you went through, and once you realize this, the sky becomes the limit.

Chapter Five: Take Care

Why taking care of your emotional and mental health through self-care strategies and external support are necessary for freedom.

Chapter Six: Love is Patient

Why you should get to know yourself before you seek love and how to grow with someone if you still carry baggage from your past.

Chapter Seven: Good Versus Better

How you can incorporate a genuine personal relationship with God in your decisions and lifestyle.

Chapter Eight: Yet

Once you reach freedom, how do you maintain it? This chapter outlines steps to preserving your freedom so you can life a life of peace and abundance.

When you get discouraged, always revisit your why for picking up or downloading this book. When you take the time to visualize personal freedom, you can enjoy the satisfaction you will feel once you've felt it for yourself. As you read, commit to relinquishing distractions and any temporary emotions that may be present in your life right now.

Remember to focus on the bottom line and when in doubt, always choose freedom – by your standard.

Let's take this journey – together. See you on the other side Queen.

Chapter One:
Layaway Life

I needed a distraction. In the winter of 2016, I was tired, burned out, and absolutely scared of my next move. A few months prior, I had mustered up the courage to leave my job in Cincinnati to start my own business. In the moment that I quit, I felt relief, but a little dose of queasiness took over me as I walked out of the door of my job for the last time. Leaving was the easy part. Figuring out how to survive and get through grad school at the same time was a different story.

When I started my entrepreneurial journey, I didn't have much of a plan, just a strong desire to succeed – whatever that meant. The day I quit my job was the day I landed my first client, and another one came soon after. For three short months, I served them through proofreading, copyediting, graphic design, social media, and anything valuable I thought that I could offer the growth of their businesses. After a while, I became overwhelmed because I realized that I could not see an end-goal for my grind. Simultaneously, my clients were facing issues in their businesses; one was running low on motivational speaking gigs and had a hard time paying me, and the other one was in the process of returning to work full-time and would not need my services once the transition was complete.

My nerves were through the roof. Here I was, twenty-five, married, accumulating student loan debt as the minutes passed, and about to be partially unemployed at the same time. Luckily, I secured a part-time teaching gig at a broadcasting school in Dayton for extra cash, but the job was forty-five minutes away from my home. I began to think that leaving my job wasn't the best decision I could have made. I couldn't understand why things were not working in my favor and why I wasn't the "overnight" success I would often see on social media.

When my circumstances eventually took a turn for the good, I learned that the understanding of difficult moments often requires patience. Conversely, there are times that we anxiously demand the answer to a phenomenon or situation that is not meant to be understood within the moment that it exists. Regardless, for the time being, we must carry on and live with what we know rather than what we seek to understand. Sometimes what we are aware of, presently, may be just enough to suffice for lack of understanding. We have to possess enough confidence to know that what is, is, and what may be unknown will reveal itself in time, whether we are prepared for the outcome or not.

So I decided to immerse myself in something, a distraction, to remove myself from negative thoughts about potentially failing as an entrepreneur. Like any average person who desires to be distracted, I got on Facebook. As I scrolled through my timeline, lost in the lives of my friends, family, and strangers, I came across a woman by the name of Kelli Prather. Kelli posted in multiple Facebook groups about her run for the United States Senate. If she secured the Democratic nomination and won the Senate, she would become the first African-American woman to become a senator in the State of Ohio. Something compelled me to stop my Facebook scroll and reach out to Kelli. She sounded like someone I could get behind.

We met at Panera Bread on the West Side of Cincinnati a few days later. I came dressed in business wear while Kelli rocked a braided updo and workout clothes. She had just come from the gym. We talked about our backgrounds, beliefs, and aspirations, and within the hour and a half we spent together; I was a part of her campaign.

Kelli joined the race for the Senate six months before the March Primary. Like me, she didn't have a plan, but she had a desire to win. One of the fundamental arguments made by her opponents and critics during the race was that Kelli lacked the firsthand political experience to run for office. What she didn't have in policy and decision-making, she made up for in her determination. One thing that is important to note is that you cannot coach or teach passion. Passion is undoubtedly a natural substance of intuition and innovation inside of you. The belief in yourself and your abilities can ultimately trump experience and ultimately make you as qualified as qualified gets.

Kelli and I began an intensive campaign. She didn't have much money. In fact, Kelli funded her entire campaign with less than a $5,000 budget, against two opponents who raised millions with endorsements from political figureheads and celebrities. Most people told Kelli that she didn't have a chance, but still, she persisted. I persisted right along with her.

The journey to the Senate was not an easy one. Within the first month of us working together, Kelli lost her campaign manager and I decided to step in. I didn't know what I was doing, but I was happy to help. We traveled around the state of Ohio to places I had never been before. We passed out business cards to any and everyone who was eligible to vote. We went to media interviews in radio, television, and print. We worked on Kelli's presence and policies if she were to become a senator.

The process became a 24-hour job and eventually, most of my free time went to the Kelli Prather for US Senate campaign.

I put my goals on the back burner because like most people, I had not yet defined my own definition of success. When you become an entrepreneur, you have to be very specific about what success looks like to you, or otherwise, you will feel as if you are always losing yourself in the grind. When I worked with Kelli, it was easy for me to see what success looked like to her: becoming a United States Senator. But for me, I couldn't tell you what my end-goal looked like. All I can say is that I wanted to become an entrepreneur and at first, that was good enough. Later on, I realized that some things prevented me from defining and achieving a level of success that felt attainable and realistic.

I was living a layaway life. If you are unfamiliar with the layaway system, it is a purchasing process created for consumers during the 1920s and 1930s around the time of the Great Depression. A layaway allowed consumers to place an item that they liked on reserve while they made regular deposits to one day make the item their own. The item was usually out of the consumer's budget so he or she would use a payment plan to get it out of the layaway. If a person didn't make regular deposits, the item was often put back on the shelf for someone else to buy, and the person typically would not get back the money he or she invested in getting the item out of the layaway.

I often refer to the layaway analogy because it is so critical to your success. Each time we lay the "thing" – success, freedom, healing, peace, self-esteem – we want "away," we delay the end gratification that we would secure if we make regular deposits. A "deposit" is the effort you put towards taking that "thing" you yearn to remove from the layaway. Without consistently making deposits, you run the risk of being a window shopper of your inner desires.

As I worked with Kelli, I slowly stopped making deposits on what I had thought was my dream. I relied on my savings and working at the school to sustain my finances; however, I temporarily immersed myself in something else to avoid the reality that I felt. Working with Kelli made me feel like I was working towards a greater good, but when it was time to think about my business, I felt like a failure. My avoidance couldn't last forever, and after March 15 I had to snap back into my reality. Ohio Democrats choose Ted Strickland as their contender to go against incumbent Republican Senator Rob Portman.

Amazingly, this didn't stop Kelli from going. She was excited about her first race, especially a statewide race that she threw her hat in at the last minute. Despite finishing at third place, Kelli garnered more than 144,000 votes, which was a little over twelve percent of the population in Ohio. When I asked her how she felt, she replied with a chuckle, "Well, you know the Cincinnati City Council race is up next. If I could do this, I know I can run for City Council."

Little does Kelli know, her unwavering confidence restored me. She was determined to have a voice in the government and continued to make deposits on her dream, despite being temporarily blocked by failure. She was clear, she was focused, and her determination was the shining light at the end of my tunnel.

After talking with Kelli, I decided to re-center myself and figure out what I was truly trying to do with my life. I peeled back the layers of my thoughts to truly understand why I couldn't define my success and it hit me: I couldn't determine my success because I still had things that were holding me back. As I tried my hardest to project confidence to the world, inside, I still dealt with things that prevented me from operating to my fullest potential. I've had multiple successes and failures, but one thing has remained constant:

My business will not operate at one hundred percent unless I am one hundred percent. It's often common for people to trudge through life without addressing the baggage that closely follows them. We normalize our issues and place ourselves in a box of unworthiness, too afraid or too oblivious of knowing that a greater life is waiting for us to find it.

Once I had the realization that I needed to do some inner healing within myself, I began to see success as more than the attainment of wealth or popularity. Success became the acquisition of personal freedom. Freedom from self-doubt. Freedom from low self-esteem. Freedom from my past.

When you are brave enough to define success for yourself, void of any of definition that may have been previously presented in your life, you experience a feeling of newness inside of you. Success on your terms is the first step to making a deposit for freedom. Defining its very core is a declaration that will give you a complete sense of independence.

But first, I had to do a holistically evaluate my life and identify the areas of repair. Since my revelation, I've lived by 5

Ps, valuable principles that have helped me put the pieces of my life back together and ultimately help take my freedom out of the layaway. They are as followed:

Develop a *plan* that allows you to stay on course but gives you wiggle room for organic life changes.

The single thing that freedom seekers have in common is consistency. Each time I outline my goals, being consistent remains top of my list. I can no longer allow self-doubt or burnout dictate how much of my potential I can reach and I have to be stronger than my temporary setbacks. It's essential to dig deep – there is always an underlying theme to our shortcomings, and I found that a lack of consistency in striving for freedom has been a detriment.

When you determine the "thing" in your life that you have been leaving in the layaway, it becomes time to create a plan to make deposits. Get clear about your intentions and motivation by creating SMARTER goals. In 2016 I created a resource called the SMARTER Goals Worksheet (You can download the sheet on skinnyblackgirlscode.com) based off of SMART goals, first introduced to the world in the November 1981 issue of Management Review by George T. Doran. The SMARTER acronym stands for **Specific, Measurable, Actionable, Realistic, Timely, Evaluative, and Refreshable**.

On the sheet, I list out the areas of life that I believe are most essential:

- Family and Friends
- Spiritual Growth

24

- Emotional Growth
- Education/Career Advancement
- Financial Growth
- Health and Wellness
- Leisure/Creativity

These are the areas of our life that allow us to be covered. When most of us create goals, we think of them from a professional, financial, health and wellness, or an educational standpoint. Holistically looking at your life will allow you make sure you are addressing all of your needs and not neglecting areas that need your attention. More often than not, people avoid the spiritual and emotional growth of their lives, because life, *is*, well, just life. It comes at us fast, whether we like it or not, and it can be hard to catch a breathe and remember to cater to the abstract elements of life that keep us grounded as individuals.

I'll give you an example of a SMARTER Goal that I had this year for the area of Emotional Growth:

Specific: Find healing from the traumatic events in my life through authentic writing and speaking engagements about my story to help other women get through their life obstacles.

Measurable: I will measure my success by writing a book and speak at an event related to empowerment and self-esteem at least once a quarter.

Actionable: I will boldly take these steps by releasing a self-published book by September 2017. I will also share my story in women's circles and on the Pink Lemonade Podcast to be scheduled as a guest speaker for other events.

Realistic: Yes

Timely: I will speak at least once a quarter: March 31, 2017, June 30, 2017, September 30, 2017, and December 31, 2017. I will release my book to the world on September 30, 2017.

Evaluative: I will adjust my self-publishing deadline if I run out of money to produce my book; however, I will still create an eBook. If I do not speak in public at an event, I will make it a mission to live stream on my platform to share my story anyway.

Refresher: When in doubt, this quote will keep me focused,

"I write for those women who do not speak, for those who do not have a voice because they were so terrified because we are taught to respect fear more than ourselves. We've been taught that silence would save us, but it won't." – Audre Lorde

Smart goals have helped me grow tremendously because unlike the flaky, non-goal oriented, entrepreneur and woman I was in the beginning; I now had things to work on. It is also important to note that as you create goals, give yourself wiggle room to adapt to change. Our goals do not always pan out the way we may necessarily like, and it is essential to be flexible. Having flexibility in how you respond to the spontaneity life offers gives you a deliverance from the stress that typically overcomes others when they are caught off guard. The sooner you accept that life is subjected to change, the better off you allow your mental health to be.

Pray **for the things you want and the things you don't understand. Clarity comes from a higher power.**

In more recent years, I have relied on prayer more than ever to help guide me in the right direction. For a large part of my life, I was stubborn and did not include God in the decision-making process. I relied on others or myself to have all of the answers when in fact, some answers will only be revealed through Divine intervention. There have been days, months, and years where I have felt lost because I was determined to find an answer on my terms. If you are struggling to gain clarity in your life, find the desire in your heart to pray. Not just once, but every single day. I've learned that it is important to pray beyond the storms that take over our lives. Pray through the good times and bad. Allow yourself to be influenced by God's wisdom and humble yourself to know that He will answer you in due time.

However, as you pray, remember to meet God halfway. You can easily miss out on a blessing if you do not take action towards the thing you are praying about. I believe that God recognizes those who make an effort for the things you desire. Take risks – calculated and worthy of his Glory – even if the outcome is uncertain. When you stop praying and stop making deposits in your life, you stop living. Always consult with God on your next steps – He will be with you all the way.

Understand the *place* you are in your life, both figuratively and literally. Determine where you need to be to execute your plan.

As I get older, I realize that I take sole responsibility for my actions and how I react to things. As much as we want people or things to behave in a particular way, it is out of our control to ensure that they do so. With that being said, live with no limitations and carry the confidence to know that you have control over YOUR life even if it feels like things are not going in your favor. Where you currently are in your life does not define you, nor does it determine your value or worth. What matters most to you is important – never allow anyone or anything take that away from you. If you are in a place in your life that feels awkward, uncomfortable, or unpleasing, know that you can change your circumstances. It first starts with understanding how much influence that place in your life has over your motivation and decisions. You must become immune to what your external environment projects on your thought-process and transform into someone who is resilient of the negative energy around you.

Pace yourself, but don't skip out on making regular and consistent deposits in your life.

I've always lived with an "on to the next one" mentality. Taking the time to grieve, celebrating accomplishments, living in special moments, and having genuine relationships - were all a blur as I matriculated through college and my early 20s. When I was a 17-year-old girl, I attended college for the first time in a dual enrollment program at Ohio Dominican University, a private Catholic school in Columbus, Ohio. The motto of the university was, "Carpe Diem" which means, "to seize the day." It took me nearly ten years to truly understand, appreciate, and incorporate that motto into my life.

Living in the moment is invaluable. As we become more ambitious and take on better jobs, opportunities, relationships, etc., it can sometimes feel overwhelming or impossible to savor the moments that we worked so hard to bring to fruition. At some point, you have to remember that your life is not a sprint; it's more of a marathon. Don't be in a race - especially if you believe that you should be on the same timeline as someone else. From the time I had my first boyfriend until the time I started my first business, I've occasionally compared my journey with someone else's journey because I felt pressured or stressed to live by where society claims I should be in my life. Give yourself permission to move at your own pace. However, do not allow moving at your own pace become an excuse for being complacent or not making moves at all. When you know what it is that you desire in your life, begin to act with a sense of urgency. If you recall, in a layaway system, when you don't make regular deposits, you run the risk of the item being taken off of the shelf or not being able to recoup the deposits you've made to get the item out of layaway. You've worked too hard not to get what you desire - make regular deposits in your life, so you live with no regrets.

Prioritize *peace*. A clear mind leads to clear decisions.

When your mind is free from disturbance, it allows you to be able to see the bigger picture. Distractions are a detriment to the mind and prevent you from making sound and well-developed decisions. For many years I lived "double-minded." My mind was always in a state of compromise because I constantly felt the need to choose between doing the right thing in my gut versus "going with the flow," which is not always the most righteous or best thing to do. My double-mindedness was often influenced by other people, who I believed had it all together, but really on the inside, they were fighting their own set of demons. The best way

29

to circumvent being at the crossroad of two completely different paths is first to outline what is most important to you in life. Then, identify the habits that remove you from operating in a space that allows you to prioritize the things that mean most to you and offers the most value. But, without peace, it can be difficult to get to a place where decision-making is easy. Prioritizing peace is an ongoing process, and as you grow, the act of peace itself may change over time. One of the first steps I took towards finding peace was setting limits for others and myself, scheduling time for myself to think and reflect about what mattered most to me, and letting go of negative emotions. Life is too short to dwell on decisions; when you develop a sense of pride and values for yourself and do not allow anything to interfere them, the decision-making process becomes a lot easier. Once you establish peace and values, stand firm in your decisions. Avoid being "wishy-washy" and do not change up your decision for the approval of others -- remember that you have to live with yourself at the end of the day.

Chapter One Reflection
1. What areas of your life have you been leaving in the layaway?
2. What does success truly mean to you?
3. How are you making regular and consistent deposits on the thing you want in life?
4. How can you use the SMARTER Goals model to help you implement the plan you have created for freedom?
5. What steps are necessary for you to achieve peace?
6. Can you relate to the 5 Ps (Plan, Pray, Pace, Place, Peace)? Are there any P's that you regularly do? Or are there any P's that you need to incorporate in your life right now?

Chapter Two:
Forgiveness is Freedom

Broken people do broken things. There are things that I have done that I am not proud of and it took a while to understand the root of my brokenness. For years, I sabotaged my ability to heal because I did not think that I was worthy of being anywhere near a state of bliss.

When unfavorable situations occur in our life, negativity consumes our thought process. *"What did I do wrong?" "Why did this happen to me?"* Those are all questions that may linger well beyond the moments we actually want to put out of our minds forever.

The question "why" is especially powerful. Each time that I asked myself "why," I often envisioned myself as a victim in some scenarios. Certainly, some situations are out of our control; however, at times, being a victim is the only way to describe a role because we may have done everything in our power to change an inevitable outcome. Unfortunately, while "why" can give us the comfort of placing blame elsewhere (or on ourselves), it locks us into a position of complacency. Without have the answer to "why," we become stagnated, stuck, and rooted in the notion that we cannot "move on" until we have a logical explanation or reason of why occurrences led to a specific result.

For nearly five years after I had an abortion, I replayed my relationship with my unborn child's father. I beat myself up, often blaming myself for not rejecting him when we first met or moving too fast to jump into a relationship. Me asking myself "why" the relationship failed and ultimately resulted in a life-changing decision that truly affected how I looked at men moving forward. It changed how I looked at myself. I was no longer a work in progress, or a carefree, positive, happy go-lucky-girl. I became ruthless, unbothered, and intentionally hurtful with my actions. I made up my mind that relationships were not for me and I had every intention to treat any man that I met with the same courtesy that given to me: none.

For a brief period, this worked. Nothing fazed me, and any time I felt the slightest possibility that I would be placed in an emotionally compromising state, I would bury myself in my academics, excessive partying, or someone else who was not a threat to captivating my attention for very long. While I hid my emotions on the outside, I was crying out on the inside, with the question, "why" still burning a hole in my conscious.

Later on, I realized that while my abortion and toxic relationship that led up to it was a wake-up call, I had been subconsciously asking myself "why" for a number of years.

I questioned my body weight and why I couldn't look like the women I saw on television.

I wondered why it was so shameful for me to be intelligent and talk "white".

I wondered why I had a gun pointed to my head on the school bus in the eighth grade because I wouldn't give a boy my phone number.

I wondered why I was sexually assaulted twice in high school and why one of the times I did not speak up for myself.

I wondered why wanting to be someone intimidated people around me.

I wondered why I needed to "code switch" in work environments and why my "normal" self did not make the cut.

I wondered why I constantly allowed people to use and abuse my talents and gifts for their own personal gain.

I wondered if I was a fraud and was truly good at the things I set out to do.

I wondered why I continued to hurt people that I loved with bad decisions that I continued to make.

I wondered why I even *existed*.

At some point, asking myself, "why" became a debilitating continuum of raw emotions that became uncontrollable. From the time I was 18 until the age of 24, I would have a series of panic attacks. Oftentimes, they stemmed from stress, Imposter Syndrome, and overexerting myself; however, many of them came from focusing on things that were out of my control. The attacks were breathtaking, and temporarily placed me into a feeling of hopelessness. They would occur anywhere; in the middle of the night, in a traffic jam, during a phone conversation – it didn't matter.

Coincidentally, as I battled suppressed demons from my past, I watched my father experience the same fate of frequent panic attacks. For most of his life, he has been consumed with the past, despite creating his own success story. He was an entrepreneur who once was a 12-year-old boy who moved from Uniontown, Alabama to Columbus, Ohio with a first-grade education and an impoverished family of ten. My dad has suffered from panic attacks for a major portion of his life, and it petrifies me that I also carry the same trait. After hearing and seeing my dad experience the same helplessness I experienced personally, I made it a priority to change the trajectory of my mindset.

Instead of asking myself "Why," I began to ask myself "how?" I must admit, it took time to ingrain this question as a mantra for my life moving forward. I had to become sick and tired of living in a past that I could not change. I was fed up with obsessively victimizing myself and using my past as a scapegoat for why I was unable to grow and become a better person.

As a highly ambitious girl, I had desires to go farther than anyone I had ever known and asking "why" would never allow me to be able to prosper. After college, I became serious about personal branding and building a brand that would standout. I've had successes and failures, but one thing has remained constant:

My brand cannot be one hundred percent unless I am one hundred percent.

Granted, I know that no one is perfect. We will all deal with obstacles throughout our life, whether they incurred externally or are self-inflicted. But it's not about how many issues we have;

34

it's about how well we manage them and how much we want to reach our goals. When I was working on my first business venture, the Barter Babes, I hired a business coach. One of the key things my coach emphasized to me was learning how to prioritize and compartmentalize to create a feeling control over my business. While I believe in the value of doing these things, I knew it would take self-reflection to make real change happen.

If you have been constantly asking yourself, "why", I have a list of ways to help you move towards a "how" mentality to help you confront your past, live in the moment, and look forward to the future:

Forgiveness is not optional; it's necessary to move on.

When I was 18-years-old, I got an abortion. For a long time, I never forgave myself. I remember graduating from high school shortly after the process, earning both a 4.0 in college and high school through a dual enrollment program called Seniors to Sophomores. A few weeks after graduation, I broke down in tears. I strived so hard to become someone, and after my abortion, it seemed like it no longer mattered. What was a 4.0 GPA to a *life*? I experienced a level of conviction that consumed my thoughts, behaviors, and actions and it made me irrational and unpredictable. I made the executive decision that I could never forgive myself and my acting out was a demonstration of this declaration. I stayed out late, would stay away from home for days, went to the club excessively, and continued to deal with my boyfriend until I learned he was cheating on me before, during, and after my abortion. I needed an escape.

Then by the grace of God, Wilberforce University happened. I felt ashamed of myself and felt like I let down my family after the news broke that I had an abortion. I was eager to get away and start anew, and what better place to seek refuge than an HBCU in the middle of nowhere? On my first visit to the campus, I went with my dad and had $200 deposit in hand for my housing deposit. I was going whether I liked the campus on not. I was going to force myself to like it no matter what. Luckily, I fell in love with the university, almost immediately.

My first semester of Wilberforce, I was introduced to God in ways I had never felt before. My mother was a devout Jehovah's Witness, and while my father believed in God, he wasn't a big churchgoer. I spent most of my life in a Kingdom Hall and never experienced other walks of worship. When I arrived at Wilberforce University, the nation's oldest private historically black college owned by the AME church, it amazed me to see so many people my age dedicated to their faith and willing to help me find mine. I visited several churches with my friends, becoming more and more comfortable with understanding that my faith was not only limited to the experiences I found within the Kingdom Hall.

During my freshman year, I was baptized at an Apostolic church in Springfield, Ohio. For the first time in months, I felt like I could find redemption, not only for my abortion, but also for other things that I experienced in my life that had subconsciously affected me. Getting baptized gave me an opportunity to experience true forgiveness, and from that moment, I've learned how to recognize those feelings of guilt as temporary, because I know that I am forgiven through the blood of Jesus Christ.

Unfortunately, getting baptized wasn't the complete end of my guilt. I struggled for a long time to truly overcome those feelings. Sometimes, I have a nightmare, or around the month of May, I cry and get depressed, often not wanting to be around children, but I persevere. One of things people never tell you about getting an abortion is the mental anguish that is experienced afterwards. For some people, they can do it, and be done. For others, like me, it can change the trajectory of their state of mind. I learned to forgive myself, whole-heartedly, even on the days where it seems like forgiveness is not an option.

Forgiveness is a precursor to personal freedom. Without forgiving others or forgiving yourself, you can never fully achieve a peace of mind. Forgiveness is sometimes not easy, but it is possible. It takes an assessment of your pride and a push for self-actualization. Abraham Maslow, a leading psychologist says in his book Motivation and Personality, "The most beautiful thing we can experience is the mysterious." The mystery of forgiveness should drive you to change. While you may not know what exists on the other side of mercy, it can be no worse than the space that you've already operated in. People who desire to be free embrace unfamiliar circumstances, no matter how much it places them outside of their comfort zone.

Learn to forgive others and do not beat yourself up about your misfortunes. Forgiveness puts you in a forward-thinking spirit and gives you the leverage to live life with the comfort of closing one door and opening a new one that leads to a freer, more satisfying life.

Self-awareness starts with being honest with yourself.

Living in a state of oblivion is the fastest way to fall into the quicksand of self-pity and self-sabotage. It is essential to learn how to be self-aware and learn your triggers. What makes you happy? What makes you sad? What makes you feel ALIVE? Oftentimes, we allow ourselves to fall into a routine of misery because it oddly becomes a place of comfort. We become afraid of moving on in fear of only returning to the same place of despair. It happens. I wish I could ensure that we could be confident and unscathed beings all of the time, but life has a funny way of rocking the boat. While the waves may seem scary, you cannot forget that every past failure, tragedy, and disappointment has undeniably prepared you for this moment. But it takes YOU to realize that you are bigger than your past. You must believe that you are exceptionally worthy of moving on and receiving the life that you deserve. It starts with acknowledging where you've been, the role you played in a situation, understanding what you need to work on, determining HOW you plan to move on and deciding WHAT you plan to do if you find yourself reverting back to a state of hopelessness.

It sounds easier said than done, but you must be ravenous for change. Change starts with the audacity to want more for your life. You must be able to look in the mirror and deem yourself worthy of change regardless of what projections your past may cast on you.

Do not allow doubt or fear to take away everything that was meant for you to have. You are not a prisoner to your past. Whatever happened, happened and there is no denying or changing it. However, you must be honest with yourself about your life's narrative to move on. You must start by first identifying where you are struggling in life and being real with yourself to truly define, redefine, and execute a plan that gets you closer to the truth. Your truth.

Sometimes, we get an inkling of ambition, and have the courage to want to be a better version of ourselves. There has been many times where I talked myself into being a badass, confident as ever, and ready to take on the world. I've accomplished amazing things, but what I considered to be amazing could have been monumental if I had taken the time to have an honest dialogue with myself about the brokenness that lingered over my head like a dark cloud. Because of not taking my issues head on, I often relied on the validation of others to complete me, talked myself out of taking action and asking for forgiveness later, and suffered from bouts of self-doubt and low self-esteem. There have been times where I've half-heartedly invested in myself. I flirted with my potential, but never went all the way because of the baggage I carried in my mind and spirit. The last thing that you should ever want to do is half-heartedly believe in yourself.

Broken people can never fully or truly operate at one hundred percent, and I can't say that enough. There will always be a lingering, unresolved, falsehood that dictates how you see yourself and how much you let yourself grow. It is hard to move forward if you are clinging to something that should no longer control you.

Take the time to create a list of everything that you've ever suppressed or avoided emotionally. Then, address those items on the list. Instead of asking yourself "why" something happened a particular way, list, "how" these things have affected opportunities or growth in your life. Next, write affirmations on how you will reevaluate your situation and eventually, and take strides to a better life.

For example, when I was younger, my father would always describe my older sister and I using the words "pretty" and "smart," but for me, those adjectives never were matched in the same sentence. I am dark skin and my older sister is light skin. I often heard my father describe my sister as the "pretty" one and me as the "smart one." Coming from the South, my father was plagued with the construct of colorism. Being light skinned was a desire. I know it was for him, as I remember him being self-conscious about his skin and using skin lighting cream when I was a child and teen.

My father's words always stuck with me. I don't think he meant harm with what he said, but I never realized until later how his words affected how I looked at myself. Of course, I was already skinny, that was enough of a problem for me in itself, but I remember too, purchasing skin lighting cream in middle school to appear lighter. I didn't like appearing in pictures if it didn't make me look like my melanin looked lighter than it appeared. If you look at my eighth-grade school picture, I was significantly "brighter" than the previous years.

About two years ago, I sat down and told my father how his words made me feel. He didn't remember, but I informed him that it hurt. I never believe that he thought I was beautiful, and as a teen and young adult, I would seek the attention of boys and men who made me feel that way. I went through a lot of heartache to be validated, but I eventually began to see beauty in myself. My high school principal was a major reason for that.

Every day, he would call all of the young women in the school beautiful. He showed us all the utmost respect, and even mentored the young men in the school to become better gentlemen. While "beautiful" was a part of my principal's everyday vocabulary, he will never know how much those words meant to me. When I talk to most people about high school, I usually hear, "Good riddance! I'm glad high school is over – worst experience of my life." For me, it was totally opposite. For most of high school, I felt empowered, beautiful, confident, and ready to take on the world and I will cherish those years for the rest of my life.

I don't know why my father never called me beautiful as a child. I am okay with that and have long forgiven him for it. But for years, I allowed being ashamed of my skin color dictate my confidence and place me in a state of desperation because I did not fit of what I had perceived to be true beauty.

When I entered college, I began to see more and more confident dark skin women emerge in mainstream media and around me. I no longer felt like I needed lighter skin to slay. I started to be comfortable in my own skin. For the first time, I would smile at myself in the mirror and tell myself I was beautiful. No validation was necessary from anyone else because I felt beautiful. It took an honest conversation with myself to understand why I didn't feel that way in the first place. But for years, I pushed my dad's words out of mind and replaced them with actions that stagnated my growth and delayed my full confidence in my appearance.

I am at peace with my skin color now. Doing the research to understand the root of this problem of colorism changed my perspective. I will not be ashamed of my skin, because that is the type of thinking that has divided African-Americans for years. I had to have an honest conversation with myself to realize the problem, and eventually, create terms that allowed myself to feel free. My black is beautiful and it needs no validation.

Learn how to detach yourself from outcomes and open your mind to possibilities.

In the summer of 2017, I was the emcee of a women's empowerment event in Cincinnati, Ohio called "Meeting in the Ladies' Room." At the event, I heard testimonies from four powerful women who allowed themselves to be vulnerable for the evening. They told deep stories that you would never know just by looking at them and their current success.

One speaker, the four-time bestselling author, Cheryl Polote-Williamson, said something that changed my life; "Purpose is where you are right now." Her words were so profound and stuck with me well beyond the event. For many of us, we are often told to find our God-given purpose to live a fulfilling life. Purpose is defined as the reason for which something is done or created or for which something exists. There are hundreds of books, TedTalks, seminars, blog posts, and podcast that advocate for finding our purpose and not settling for anything less.

When I heard Cheryl speak, it changed my entire outlook about purpose. Purpose once seemed like a destination, but now it feels like a series of moments intertwined in an infinite path of trial, error, and self-evolution. In retrospect, it was almost as if purpose was a singular outcome. Everyone is put on this earth to do ONE thing...right? I would disagree, now. Right now, you are operating in a moment that is intentionally set up in your life to get you to the next element of your purpose. While purpose may appear to be warm and fuzzy noun that gives insurmountable feelings of satisfaction and completeness, I realize that purpose is embedded in every good and bad experience that you will ever go through in your life. Purpose is a teacher - when turmoil hits your life, it isn't just for any reason. You were meant to experience one thing to get to the next place that was meant for you to experience. It is important to note that the faster that we realize that life will have challenges and obstacles the better equipped we are to handle them when they transpire.

At the time of this writing, I am 26-years-old. While many of my peers have it together, I am only beginning to figure out what makes me an asset to the world.

I lived the early part of my 20s searching for purpose. I went to college to find it in mass media. I worked in multiple different industries to find my niche. I've started businesses to see if it was truly for me.

Each time that I started something new, I found a hint of hesitancy in my decision. While searching for my purpose, I felt disappointed at times, often comparing myself to others or worrying that I wasn't as far ahead in life as I should be. The disappointment I possessed contributed to my brokenness – I had a broken spirit and broken confidence about who I was as a person and what value I brought to the world.

After hearing Cheryl speak, I realized that I no longer needed to have those feelings. I had to reevaluate the difference between failure and my being too hard on myself. Regardless; I wasn't straying away from my purpose, I was living in it. Purpose is being bold. Purpose is about getting up and trying even when you have the slightest doubt in yourself. These moments, no matter how terrifying or satisfying they may be, are propelling you to go forward.

I recently read a book called the Law of Attraction Made Easy by Meera Lester. One of the best takeaways I got from the book was to begin detaching myself from outcomes. It is so easy to focus on one very specific result when you believe that you have wholeheartedly put in the work and are deserving of that particular outcome. Unfortunately, outcomes are not always what we expect them to be and we must learn how to accept it.

For example, when I graduated from college, I was determined to work in a newsroom. Throughout my entire life, I wanted to become a television journalist and I landed an opportunity in Cincinnati to work for a local news station. At the station, I was a digital content producer where I wrote stories for the web and handled social media. At first, I enjoyed my job - I was on the breaking edge of digital media becoming a big part of the newsroom and didn't even know it. Unfortunately, while I enjoyed learning all I could about the web, the newsroom was not for me. The work hours were crazy, the environment often left me stressed and my colleagues were very direct, and sometimes condescending. I cried in the bathroom one evening and realized that the outcome that I thought I would have (i.e. being happy and working in a news station) was not a reality. I contemplated for weeks if I should quit my job because I had spent the last four years of college preparing for what I thought was my big moment.

Looking back, I realized that working at that TV station was a big moment. It taught me about myself and stretched me in ways I would have never experienced if I hadn't taken the chance to move to Cincinnati to follow what I thought was my calling. It was a moment that has come and gone, but it prepared me with the training in social media for many other successes I had experienced within four years of leaving the station. If I had dwelled on this experience for too long, it would have never gotten me to this point today.

Remember, no pain is forever. While it pained me to go in a different direction, I've never regretted my decision or any that followed when it came finding my purpose. Sure, there are days that I question what I am doing, but Cheryl's words helped me realize that I am doing everything I am supposed to be doing at this moment.

If you are attached to an outcome – stop. Say yes to give yourself the flexibility to grow and learn outside of your regular thinking and whatever preconceptions you have about purpose. While I am a proponent of mapping your life, vision board parties, etc. I also carry the belief to let life happen organically and live in each moment as they come. I've suffered from disappointment that derives from perfectionism and Imposter Syndrome and I am here to tell you to free yourself from those debilitating conditions. We are all a work in progress; so, embrace your progress and know that each step is indicative that you are exactly where you are supposed to be in life. Don't let anyone tell you any different.

You are fully responsible for what you attract and speak in your life.

When I was in the eighth grade, I had a reading teacher by the name of Ms. Hawkins. Ms. Hawkins was no joke and appeared to think we were irresponsible 18-year-old college students instead of awkward 13-year-old middle-schoolers. Every day, we would complain about the amount of work we had to complete and she would always say, "I'm getting you ready for college. When you get to college you will be ready and you'll thank me then."

Up until that point, I had never thought of going to college. The eighth grade was the first time I learned about college and once I knew what it was and the possibilities it would bring to my life, I told myself that I would go -- not just for a bachelor's. My goal was to go all the way and be a part of the three percent of people who earn PhDs. Until this day that is still the goal. I am two-thirds of the way there, and if God is willing, I will get there by the time I am 35.

Later, I realized Ms. Hawkins was not just tormenting us with long assignments; she was planting a seed with her words. Many of my classmates and I did not have immediately family members with two or four-year degrees. She was instilling the belief that we were capable and able to attend college and she got the ball rolling before we got into high school and were blind-sided by SAT and ACT preps, college tours, and scholarship essays. Now granted, I know that other "affluent" school districts had probably been instilling college since Pre-K, but as public-school kids, we were extremely lucky to have a teacher who taught us to look beyond our current environment.

Mrs. Hawkins spoke life into us and fortunately, I had many other teachers who did the same as I went on to high school and college.

When I became an adult, I had to learn how to speak life into myself, which was one of the hardest things to do in the world. For many years, I underestimated the power of my words. It still leaves me in awe that self-doubt and a lack of confidence can cross over to the messages that you verbally and physically project to the world. As a recurring theme of this chapter, I discuss the question "why" versus "how". Self-limiting thoughts exist beyond the "why" factor and it is important that you learn how to identify when you are asking yourself questions that set you back and do not allow you to move forward.

Putting things off out loud used to be a regular part of my vocabulary. After my ambition left me feeling broken, I would often get reenergized with ideas and share them. When someone would ask me when it was time to execute, I would say, "Oh, I'll get to it tomorrow," or "I'll get to it next week." Later, I heard someone say that you are arrogant if you think you have the luxury of tomorrow to do what you should have accomplished today.

That got my attention quickly.

When you feel broken, you put off your potential, as if you have all the time in the world to dwell in the past. While brokenness may be an excuse for a lack of execution, you must remember that being broken can no longer be a scapegoat if you desire a genuine level of personal freedom in your life. Sometimes, what we put off today, we put off forever.

So what did I do? I changed my language. I put a date on my actions to ensure that I talked the talk. I surrounded myself with like-minded people who would not allow me to engage in self-limiting thoughts that would sabotage my success and growth as a woman. I started to purge my social media feeds and only subjected myself to things that related to positivity, innovation, happiness, and getting ahead. I consciously started to evaluate my language - from the way I spoke to others face-to-face to how I responded to an email.

You must have the willpower to speak life over yourself. Whether you realize it or not, your life depends on every word, syllable, and phoneme that leaves your lips. There are a multitude of words that you can eliminate from your vocabulary. Here are a few that I consciously recognized that hindered my growth and I continue to watch out for to speak confidently about my endeavors and myself:

Can't

The word "can't" is the root of all evil. When you say you can't do something, you are telling someone that you are passively creating limitations for yourself. You are not being direct, as opposed to saying that you "won't" do something - because people will know your exact intentions. The word "can't" is largely associated with the fear of failure or rejection and it is important for me to use this word sparingly. When I feel myself saying I can't, I ask myself, "Is it truly something I cannot do because I lack the skill? Or is it because I am scared?" Always opt to test your limits and use this word sparingly, if even, at all.

Sorry

At one point in my life, I felt like I said sorry at least fifteen times a day. It was so bad, I would apologize for sneezing, a natural reaction that no human being should ever apologize for doing. Saying "sorry" unnecessarily can put you in a vulnerable place of being perceived as weak or a pushover. Regardless of if you are in a relationship or at work, you should only apologize when it is truly a reason to say you're sorry. For example, I created a report for my boss and submitted it to him for approval. As I watched him go over my work, I blurted out, "I'm sorry if I went overboard with the descriptions and the charts....." and before I went any further he told stopped me and said, "Don't ever apologize for doing your job." When I thought about it, I wondered why I did apologize for doing good work? After all, that is why he hired me, right? My "sorrys" were often rooted in the anxiety of perfectionism. Before I stopped truly caring about what others thought of me, I would apologize for being me. That's a no-no. Reevaluate why you say you're sorry and brainstorm how you can eliminate this language in your communication. Freedom requires a clear conscious that is free from extending itself to pointless apologies.

Hopefully/Try

I placed "hopefully and try" in the same category because they both give off a friendly stench of doubt. When I say "hopefully" something will happen, there is a small part of me that thinks that something won't happen at all. When you want something to happen you must speak it into existence. If it doesn't happen, you must realize that it was not meant to be (to your standards) and the overall outcome is still connected to your purpose. It may not be apparent immediately, but as I mentioned before, each step we take in life is connected to our calling.

Trying is akin to hopefully; because it says that I may or may not do something. I may or may not give it my all. I may or may not believe I can even do it. If I am going to "try" to do something, it ranks at the bottom of my priorities. I replaced trying with "I am" statements. "I am going publish this book in September" sounds way more action-oriented than "I am going to try to publish this book by September." Saying "Hopefully, my book will be a best-seller" would never trump, "My book will be a best-seller." Eliminate both words from your vocabulary altogether. They stop you from fully believing in yourself and open you up to doubts that have no place in your mind.

Think

I reduced my intelligence many times with the word "think". There are times when I knew that I had a perfect solution, but when I presented my ideas, I said, "I think I may have a solution" or "I think I may be right about this, but..." When you say you think, you immediately discredit your own thoughts. You seem unsure and unconfident. I'll give you an example. What if someone told you, "I think I love you." While you may be flattered, you might ponder why they just didn't flat out say, "I love you." The word "think" brings a wishy-washy feeling to a conversation and you want to always say what you mean and mean what you say. When you know something is real or have a fantastic idea, say it with confidence and don't allow "think" to creep into your vocabulary and affect how others perceive your certainty.

Learn how to identify the words that weaken your speech and replace them with words that make you feel confident and comfortable. As I've learned, you will have to learn how to be your biggest cheerleader in this journey to freedom, and I say that both figuratively and literally. A cheerleader's role is to be positive, enthusiastic, and vocal with support, and you must do these things for yourself internally and externally to thrive and be a master of your words and lifestyle.

Chapter Two Reflection
1. Who in your life have you not forgiven? Why?
2. Have you been able to forgive yourself? What is stopping you from doing it?
3. What negative words are you speaking into your life?
4. How will you detach yourself from outcomes?
5. Do you feel as if you are living in your purpose right now? If not, what will you do to change it?
6. When is the last time you were honest with yourself about your feelings?

Chapter Three:
My Size Does Not Define My Worth

When I first began the concept of the Skinny Black Girl's Code, I remember having a very candid conversation with my dad in his living room in 2014 on a December evening. I lived in Cincinnati at the time and decided to come up for a family visit. As we sat on his soft, suede couch drinking juice (me) and beer (him), with 1950s Westerns quietly playing in the background, I excitedly tell my dad that I had recently started website for skinny black girls.

"Skinny black girls" he scoffed. "They don't have any problems, Whitney. Why don't you spend your time doing something else?"

My excitement quickly turned into defensiveness.

By this time, I had about four stories under my belt from women who were shared their personal stories with me about growing up and being bullied, ridiculed, and rejected because of their small frames. Within seconds of him making his comment, I gave him specific examples and excerpts from the stories I had collected faster than a Divine Nine pledge spitting information to his line brothers. Unfortunately, my dad wasn't convinced with my case studies by the end of my closing statements.

"I still think you could be doing something else," he said casually as he took a sip of his Blue Moon. "I'm telling you, skinny black girl's ain't got no problems."

Instead of protesting, I decided to take my dad's advice and do "something else": research.

Criticism is no new obstacle for me when it comes to the Skinny Black Girl's Code. More times than I can count, I have been asked why I created this platform and what problems do skinny black girls actually have because being skinny is a privilege (You should see my fingers air quote as I type.) In some cases, "skinny privilege" is very real based on whose cultural standard of beauty you are following.

Through countless hours of reading and surfing the Internet, I've come to learn that body image is a social construct. For years, I watched television shows, saw magazines in the grocery aisles, and witnessed mainstream movies that often didn't include darker shades of melanin or different body types. As I got older and became more acquainted with the world outside of the United States, I learned that the Western standard of beauty "white and skinny" is not ubiquitously unanimous. There is no "one-size-fits-all" for body type; other cultures value and celebrate a variety body types for different reasons.

Bigger is Better...Right?

Academic research and self-esteem support resources for African-American women and girls who identify themselves as "skinny" are extremely limited. As I was going through my season of low-self esteem as a young adult, I tried to look up resources that could help. I came across a few blogs from women who shared their experience, but never found anything by a professional organization that addressed the things that I was feeling. Mostly, when it came to being skinny, the only resources available were for anorexia and bulimia, which is often coined as the "White Girl problems" in the black community.

My problems were the total opposite. I was determined to find a Jesus and cornbread diet that could rebuke the small body I felt like I had been cursed with from a teen onward. I ate everything I could get my hands on with hopes of becoming more shapely to emulate the women I thought were attractive or that the boys my age wanted to date.

Fortunately for me, my genetics worked against me, cursing the very essence of my journey's existence. I wanted to be thick. There was no if, and's nor but's about it. Bigger equaled better and that's what exactly I was going to get.

See, I wanted to be normal a black girl with a chance to blend in with the crowd. I could empathize with girls who were heavier than thick and stuck out like a sore thumb—I did too. When you're skinny, your "sick", "anorexic" or extremely fit. You're never just normal. When you're skinny you can't help but wonder what normal feels like. Skinny equates extreme flaws or highly desirable assets, depending on whom you talk to.

Time after time, I've heard, "I wish I could be skinny like you. You're lucky!" "Here!" I scream in my head. "Take it!"

Instead of expressing the un-obvious, I smiled with a fake confidence of a body I can't change. I mostly get those reactions from white women. I think they like skin and bones I'm in. I can fit a size four easily but when I looked in the mirror, it didn't seem fair. I was stuck in another woman's fantasy body.

Later on, when I was pursuing my Master's Degree and re-exploring the topic for this book, I found that I was not alone. Initially, most of the research I found examined self-esteem among African-Americans women and teens, focusing on matters like premature sexuality, substance abuse, pregnancy, and identity confusion. Several studies prove that many black women are content with their size, with the exception of women who identify as skinny in the black community.

While it is not commonly discussed, being a full-figured woman has dominated the African-American standard of beauty for hundreds of years. In the book, Fat History: Bodies and the Beauty in the Modern West by Peter N. Steams, a historical context of the black female body is explored in a short, but informative chapter entitled, "The African-American Alternative: Power and Size."

Traditionally, black women who were larger in stature were provided with more respect and praised for their body types. A fuller body type indicated strength and a position of power in many African countries. According to Teaching Tolerance, a project of the Southern Poverty Law Center, African women engaged in "fattening periods." This process slated to help women increase their beauty and chances of fertility.

In the sixth grade I met a girl who would eventually become a lifelong friend, Vicrina. Vicrina was skinny, Sierra Leonean, and very conscious of her size by default because the first line of attack from our peers was often her about weight.

Vicrina is still very skinny until this day, told me about her experience growing up skinny and African when I approached her about being featured in the Skinny Black Girl's Code.

"Growing up a skinny African girl was tough due to the fact that I didn't have the typical curvy, "thick" body African women are known for," she says. "Being teased by both Africans and African Americans made me feel like I didn't belong anywhere."

For three long years, I watched Vicrina, finesse comments about her weight. She was strong and was never short of a witty comeback to the boys and girls who came at her sideways. She may have been 5'4, less than 100 pounds, and size zero, but she never allowed anyone to push her around even if they made her feel bad on the inside. I always admired her for that.

Now Vicrina lives in New York City and works in the fashion industry for a major retailer and produces her own web-based show, called Vicrina En Vogue. The very frame she was ridiculed about in our early years is now praised and honored by others. She's done modeling gigs and has appeared in major publications because of her bold and lively style that derives primarily from the confidence she had no choice but to build when we were growing up. I consider Vicrina the true definition of skinny and savage.

Body Type and Slavery

Being "thick," particularly during the era of slavery, was an accomplishment. For white slave owners, a black woman with a fuller body type represented a woman who could endure hard and physical labor. Consequently, smaller women were often overlooked or not viewed on the same level as their thicker counterparts by their current potential or slave owners.

During slavery, the historical notion of the "Black Jezebel" was streamlined as a campaign to dehumanize and sexualize black women.

Researchers from Southern Illinois University, the University of South Carolina, and Post University, explore this phenomena to understand its long-term impact on black women today, and unfortunately, 300-some odd years later, this phenomena is alive and well. It's no secret that hip-hop culture has further extended the lifeline of sexualizing black female bodies. I would be a liar if I said that I didn't drink the Kool-Aid; I was introduced to hip-hop music and at first, unknowingly absorbed the sexually explosive culture that came with it in the early 2000s. I remember it like it was yesterday. I entered the six grade introverted, four-eyed, nerdy, and *(sigh)* skinny. I didn't wear name brand clothing and had just recently started to get relaxers in my hair a year before. Many of my female classmates didn't waste any time emulating the models and video vixens we would see on BET. They would get their hair done, nails done, and find the tightest jersey dresses and booty shorts to show off their budding (and in some cases, fully developed) assets.

Eight years before I entered middle school, Ebony magazine published a controversial article called, "Why Bigger is Better." The writer interviewed several men about their dating preferences, including the 1993 Ebony Bachelor of the Year, Keith Ridley. The 27-year-old bachelor had it made; Keith was a relatively handsome, a college graduate, and the president and operations manager of a family funeral business. Who wouldn't want to date him, right? During Keith's interview, he made a comment that stuck with me:

> "The only thing a thin woman can do for me is introduce me to a woman of size. I've never been attracted to thin or even averaged-sized sisters. I need a woman I can hold on to. Truth be told, my ideal woman is a size 20."

Keith's sentiments echoed familiar statements I've heard by boys and men all of my life. Bigger is better for some, and in the process my little skinny feelings would get hurt because I was caught up in body biases that were out of my control. I'd try to take control by plotting ways to become a bigger, thicker, reflection of what I believed was the ideal body size. Unfortunately, my body stayed in small mode for most of my teens and early 20s and that reflection never became my reality.

Skinny Shaming is the New Black

As I navigated through the pitfalls of young adulthood, I began to take note of how skinny shaming began to take form. Most specifically, I remember hearing the widely controversial song Anaconda by Nicki Minaj in 2014. Nicki Minaj has a part at the end of the song, where she shames the "skinny b*tches" in the club and praises all thick women for their assets.

As I listened to the song, I couldn't help but think about how the fourteen-year-old Whitney would have reacted. That version of me would have idolized Nicki Minaj and all of her surgery because she was the epitome of what I thought boys and men wanted.

Similarly, a few months before Anaconda took over the airways, pop singer Meghan Trainer took a few shots at skinny women in her single, "All About that Bass." Like Nicki, Meghan refers to women as skinny "b*tches" and proceeds that men like women with a butt that they can hold on to at night.

And they thought rap music was the only genre that reduced the worth of female bodies. The subtle, but often blatant, occurrences of skinny shaming in music and mainstream media are everyday realities are laughed at, overlooked, or entirely misunderstood.

For example, in 2016, I wrote a blog post outlining some of the things I've heard that were offensive to me or other skinny black girls I've met over the years. The comments go something like this:

"You need to put some meat on your bones."
"What are you complaining for? You can fit anything."
"You're shaped like a white girl."
"You're so skinny for a black girl."
"Exercise? I don't know what you are going to the gym."
"Diet? Girl, you don't need to lose any more weight or you'll disappear."
You are too small. I only date thick girls.
Skinny girls can't cook.
Insult + with your skinny a**............

Some may argue that some of these statements aren't offensive or demeaning. But you would have to be on the other side of the spectrum to know how the comments feel. It is easy to blow off what we do know or what we have not experienced.

59

When someone has low self-esteem, these kinds of comments can be damaging, no matter how old you are.

Several years ago, I worked in Cincinnati for a company. I was in one of my first "big girl" positions and had created the presentation of the century. I was so prepared that I was over prepared. In the meeting, I was the youngest, and the only African-American woman in the room. As it got around to my turn to speak, a colleague made a joke about why I wouldn't eat a donut.

"You don't want this donut, Whit? It looks like you need one," he joked as he cut his eyes at me up and down. The room erupted into laughter as I sat there unamused and super embarrassed.

Secretly, I get nervous a right before a presentation or speaking so I typically go without a meal or snack until the job was done. Eating before presenting makes me feel queasy.

Instead of giving him a tongue lashing, my first initial instinct, I focused on giving my presentation. I was slightly flustered, oddly. Comments like that hadn't bothered me for some time, so I wondered why it affected me so much.

At the conclusion of my presentation, my colleagues passed the donut box around once more. Each person had his or her helping as I talked and there was one left. As my boss reached for it, a fifty-something Sandy hair Caucasian woman, the fake comedian….er…..colleague said, "You sure you don't want to save that for Whitney? She might need it more than you do."

My boss sat back and smiled as the others in the room had a chuckle. I managed to drag through the rest of the meeting, dejected and downright ashamed. Even after graduating with college with an extremely high GPA, doing great work in my community, and creating milestones at my company, my body was still the focus of someone's joke. Needless to say, after that day I mapped out my exit. If I can't feel confident and comfortable in my work environment it's a problem. The funny thing about all this is, that if you were to ask my former colleague today about his comments, he would likely say that it was all fun and games, a natural response from most people who passively bully women about their body weight everyday. But to the person receiving the comments, fun and games are the last thing on their mind. They are thinking about what clothes can they wear to make their assets enhanced or what food or product can help them gain the most weight. When someone's appearance is attacked without a solid actualization of self or value, they become absorbed in "fixing" their flaws. For years, I was obsessed with things I could not change about my appearance, and that obsession temporarily blocked my focus on things that were actually in my control. Skinny shaming is more than YouTube trolls and passive aggressive words in a boardroom – it's a verbal cancer that leaves a residue of low confidence in your conscious. That's why, no matter who you are or how you look, be careful of what you speak into the minds of others. While you may think that your words are innocent or fun, it can cause irreversible damage to someone's self-esteem.

Love Yours

I was once the girl who did everything she could to attain a body that God did not intend for her to have. Now I am the woman who loves everything about her self - flaws and all. I'm on a mission to make sure all the women and girls around me feel what took me too long to value: confidence. Love what you see looking back at you in the mirror - it's the first step to the rest of your life.

For some women extreme body issues will never occur in their lives. For others, like me, it takes a little more umph, to be more than okay with your body. The day I decided that enough was enough was when I was a sophomore in college. I was tired of overeating to gain weight, praying for a bigger butt, and not being satisfied with myself. I decided that it was time for me stop fearing what life was like without, and focus on a life that included what I already had. I had become so frustrated with trying to be someone that God had not ordained for me to be.

When you embrace your body, you move with an entirely different confidence. When I made the declaration to myself that I would be the number one fan of my body, people could see it. Even if they didn't notice, it felt good to love me for me... "flaws" and all.

Body Image Challenge

If you have struggled to accept your body, understand that self-body acceptance is one of the most crucial things you need to do to achieve freedom. Whether you are a skinny black girl or not, it is important to be excited with what you see in the mirror. Without complete confidence in your body, it can impact confidence in other areas of your life where it matters the most. For example, if you are ashamed of your weight and have to make presentations, it will be extremely uncomfortable to present because in the back of your mind you may be wondering if everyone is really listening to you or focusing on your body.

It's time to get comfortable with being uncomfortable. As I close this chapter, I invite you to commit to a three-day body acceptance exercise that I created to help you become more comfortable with your body so you can fully achieve the personal freedom you deserve. Feel free to share the results of the challenge with me at skinnyblackgirlscode.com or on social media using the hashtag #LoveYours; I hope it changes your life as much as it changed mine.

You can download the sheets referenced in the exercises for free at www.skinnyblackgirlscode.com.

DAY ONE – Naked

Items Needed
- Full length mirror
- Likes/Dislikes Sheet
- Pencil/Pen

Challenge

Look at yourself without clothes in front of a full-length mirror for ten minutes without distractions. Study the reflection looking back at you. If it is challenging to look at yourself or certain parts of your body, make note of what makes you uncomfortable. If there are attributes that you absolutely love about yourself, list them on the opposite side of your Likes/Dislikes Sheet.

Questions:

1. Compare likes to dislikes. Which section contains more tally marks than the other?
2. Why do the items on the right make you feel uncomfortable? Have you attempted to change or alter these attributes?
3. Why do you love the attributes on the left? Are the attributes something that people often highlight about you or are they attributes that you take pride in on your own?

DAY TWO – The Good, the Bad, the Ugly

Items Needed
- Computer/Mobile Device
- Free Pinterest Account
- Internet

Challenge

Sticks and stones may break my bones but words will never hurt me...right? Using sticky notes, place one color on each of your four walls. Divide the walls by the following categories:

- Positive Comments Someone Has Said to You
- Negative Comments Someone Has Said to You
- Positive Comments You Have Made to Someone Else
- Negative Comments You Have Made to Someone Else

Questions:

1. Did you see more positive or negatives in each category? Did it surprise you?

2. When someone gives you a compliment, how does it make you feel?
3. When is the last time that you complimented yourself?
4. When someone says something negative to you, how does it impact your behavior?
5. When you say negative things to other people are you being negative because you have unaddressed issues in your life?

DAY THREE – Beauty by Your Terms

Items Needed

- Computer/Mobile Device
- Free Pinterest Account or White Board
- Internet
- Magazines

Challenge

What is your definition of beauty? In this challenge, you will define the elements that create "beauty" from your perspective. The definition of beauty can be expressed through words, images, colors, people, places, etc. Choose a minimum of five elements to represent beauty. Once you choose the images, create a Pinterest board to show your definition of beauty. Screenshot your definition of beauty and share with the Skinny Black Girl's Code on Instagram, Facebook, or Twitter, using the hashtag #LoveYours. Or if you need a reminder, purchase a white board and cut out images from a magazine and hang it up in your house as a reminder.

Questions:
1. Do you think your definition of beauty matches societies standards? Why or why not?
2. Has your definition of beauty evolved over time? How?
3. Name 3-5 people that you believe are beautiful. Why are so attracted to them?
4. What are the non-physical characteristics that make someone beautiful? List at least 5-10.

Reflection

Once you complete each exercise, do the following things over the next 30 days:

- **Leave up the positive compliments people have made about you on your wall.** Each morning before you start your day, read them.
- **Begin to keep a mental list of negative things that you say to yourself, everyday.** When you write them down, follow up with a way to turn your negative thought into a positive affirmation and put your new affirmation on a sticky note on the wall.
- **Cleanse your social media timeline.** If something makes you feel negative or unsure about yourself, unfollow or unfriend the person or page. Challenge yourself to find 3-5 accounts that help you feel good about yourself when you scroll through your timeline.
- **Wear clothes that make you feel inspired at least once a week.** You can feel a difference in your mood when you wear a cute outfit versus something you throw on for the heck of it.
- **Invest in self care.** Get a facial, get your nails done, work out to get your adrenaline pumping! Taking care of

yourself helps you feel tremendously better about yourself.

- **Immerse yourself in a cause.** When you are passionate about something dear to your heart, you don't have time to worry about body image.
- **Rely on your faith.** If you are a spiritual person be assured that God created you in his image. He doesn't make mistakes, so don't allow your own self-limiting perspective or others make you think otherwise.
- **If you don't love your body for any other reason, do it for your health.** There is evidence that suggests that the animosity that you have towards your body can lead to life-threatening health issues. Challenge yourself to compliment the parts of your body that you don't like. The more you do it, the more you will believe it.

As you move forward, remember, your size does not define your worth. You are amazing as a size zero or a size twenty. You are in control of how you feel about you. Love yourself with all that you have – self-love is freedom.

Chapter Four:
Worthy as F***

I won't apologize for using the f-word as a precursor in my chapter. I know for some, cursing is rather obscene; however, for the purpose of this micro-dissertation, it's necessary. Sometimes, the most eloquent of words cannot capture the emotion that profanity perfectly embodies. For the last two years, I've tried to eliminate curse words from my speech, and I have had the worst time doing so. When you do something that's so natural and so instinctive, you almost have to question where it all started to make progress on elimination.

I grew up in an age where it was unheard of to look "soft" – even for a young girl. Girls were unafraid, unapologetic, and ready to take on the world without a worry of who they stepped on or over along the way. We slung the word, "bitch" around like a rag doll, using the inflection of our voice to let you know if it was a term of endearment or fighting words. My mother never cursed, and until this day, I've only ever heard her say, "damn" which hardly constitutes a dirty word. I remember cursing for the first time in the fifth grade on the playground at Cassidy Elementary School. A few friends and I were under the "Eagle's Nest", a piece of playground equipment. The conversation went like this:

Friend: Whitney, you don't ever cuss.
Whitney: I cuss! (Lying, of course, but we aren't going to tell anybody).
Friend: I've never heard you say a cuss word. Say something.
Whitney: Shit.

(Laughter erupts and we go back to being happy-go-lucky 10-year-olds with newly found potty-mouths).

At that moment, I felt rebellious, free even. I never thought about even mumbling a cuss word, let alone saying one out loud. While my mother didn't curse, my father cussed like a sailor. He had no filter, and the words he said would intrigue me. My parents were divorced, and they couldn't have been more opposite of one another. I spent time with dad on the weekends and some evenings, and the things he would say were exciting because I never heard them on a regular basis. I listened to NSYNC, The Backstreet Boys, and a plethora of music from the 1950s because I was pretty much forbidden to listen to the hip-hop radio station until middle school. My mother is a devout Jehovah's Witness and she is true to its doctrine. So, my dad was a fresh of breath air and a representative of the "worldly" life that my mother tried so hard to protect me and my other siblings from living.

Although I was attracted to curse words, vulgar language didn't become a regular part of my vocabulary until a year later. Why? Life got real. The bullying nature of my classmates forced me to be hardcore even when I didn't want to be. My goal was never to be cool; I just wanted to survive the day-to-day. Middle school was a soap opera saga that never seemed to slow down. Fights, neighborhood beefs, boyfriend and girlfriend drama, fake friends, weed, generic Blood versus Crips beef, urban fashion, and hip-hop culture dominated our attention. I managed to be a good student, and it didn't go unnoticed by my teachers -- or my peers:

*"Oh, you think you smart, b****?!"*
"You talk like a white girl!"
"Let me see your paper! I know you got all the answers."
"Teacher's pet!"

I felt like being smart was my only advantage. It was the only thing that no one could ever take away from me, so I never allowed anyone to take away the confidence I had in my intelligence. When people had something negative to say, I would work harder and push myself to excel. I would allow my curiosity to lead me to books where I would learn concepts and eventually develop my own view of the world. I can honestly say I was beyond my time.

Embracing my genius was as far as my confidence went. Middle school was a very tense and stressful season in my life where I allowed my fear of being cast as a "lame" dictate decisions that I made. Later, I realized people could sense of lack of confidence and desperation to fit in.

One of the most embarrassing displays of this lack of confidence was in the seventh grade. I joined the girls' junior varsity volleyball team, despite having no athletic ability. Playing sports seemed like a great way to bond and make friends, and I was determined to use it as a vehicle to do just that. During practice one day, I recall telling some of the girls about a guy I had recently started talking to through AOL Instant Messenger (AIM). He was a few years older than I, and it was getting to a point where I was thinking about losing my virginity. This was the first guy I became "involved" with, and I would eat up his words. I was desperate for attention, and when he gave it to me, I talked about it on the highest pedestal. When you play a

70

sport, it's almost like a sisterhood or sorority. I felt like the girls on the team had my back, and they would keep my most intimate secrets.

Sike. This was so far from the truth. About a week and a half later, our coach, who was also my seventh-grade math teacher, Ms. Thompson asked me to speak with her in the hallway. As my teammates were practicing, she led me to an area out of earshot, and asked, straight up, "Are you pregnant?" with the most serious expression.

"No," I responded almost immediately, offended. What gave her the right to ask me this question? Where did this even come from? Later, I concluded that the teammates I confided in, who were also her "children," told her. Ms. Thompson was very divisive and you would clearly know if you were one of her favorites or someone who was just taking up valuable air at her school.

"Whitney," she said, in the most accusing tone ever. "I've been watching you flirt with boys in the hallway and people keep coming to me with concerns. You're pregnant."

"I'm not...." I began, but never made it to the rest of my sentence. Ms. Thompson quickly lifted my t-shirt and pointed at my stomach. Ms. Thompson was a tall woman and at least 200 pounds. She had a strong personality and demanding presence that people either loved or hated, and at that very moment, I hated the shit out of her.

"Yes, you are!" she said in a voice just barely shy of a scream. "Just look at your stomach. It's not the same size that it was before. You have a pouch. It's protruding!"

She was right. I did have a little pudge. But it wasn't from a baby. It was from the excessive and overeating I had started to engage in over the last year attempting to get "thick." I felt underdeveloped and ugly in middle school. I was so determined to get away from being skinny that I ate anything I could get my hands on that would help me gain weight. French fries. Cornbread. Fried Chicken. Bacon. McDonald's. All of that. You name it, I ate it. Ms. Thompson' inappropriate display of "concern" left my "thickness regiment" project exposed and misconstrued. I wasn't having sex; I just wanted to have a body that I could love.

"I'm not, I repeated," almost in a wail. I felt hot and uncomfortable. I couldn't even look her in the eye because I felt intimidated. I did not want to be there. She was scaring me. She made me feel a degree of embarrassment I hadn't reached before. Here I was, a few months shy of becoming thirteen and not yet even sexually active. I was being judged and type-casted into someone that I had not yet become. I say, "not yet" because once I went through Ms. Thompson' interrogation process, I became depressed, and eventually, did start to have sex. People already thought that I was, so what did it matter if I did or did not? I remember, a few years before the shirt-lifting fiasco, I had a "friend" in elementary school tell me in the fifth grade that she thought I would become pregnant in high school. When I asked her why, she said, "Because, you just seem like the type." We made a bet, and I was determined to prove her wrong. But later, I learned, that life has a profound way of proving *me* wrong.

72

The only people I told about feeling violated by Ms. Thompson were my close friends, Annie and Vicrina. I never told my parents or any other adults. I felt that because she was an adult, especially one with authority at the school, I had to accept her narrative of me. I had not yet reached the level of emotional intelligence that allowed me to say, "f*** Ms. Thompson and whatever she said or thought about me". She will never know the emotional anguish I experienced that moment in the hallway, and after that day, I never looked at her the same. I dreaded going to her class, literally counting down the seconds from when it started until the next period bell would ring. My self-esteem was shot, and I was constantly paranoid about not only what people thought about my body but also what people thought about me as a person.

This anxiety followed me throughout the rest of middle school. My father once told me, "Girl, you are going to have haters all your life, so I suggest you get used to it." I was such a young and vulnerable girl when he said it, but his words instantly became clear after that moment.

Sometimes I wish I could have skipped those three long years and gone straight to high school from elementary school. However, I know that if I hadn't endured those years of awkwardness, embarrassment, bullying, I would not have become the person that I am.

Although I had so much resentment about my looks, little did I know, I was rapidly growing into them. Boys began to pay attention to me in ways I had not experienced before. Unfortunately, their girlfriends and crushes did too. As much as I wanted to keep a low profile at school, my name became second nature in everyone's mouth after I was betrayed by my teammates. Not only did they tell Ms. Thompson, they told other people in the school, too. I can't count the number of times that I saw people whisper about me, or had friends (and bullies), tell me about things that were being said about me in middle school. I began to skip school frequently to escape the nightmare that school was becoming for me. So many people talked about me, sometimes to my face, and tried to shut down my self-esteem. It wasn't very high to begin with, so what little pride I had within myself was shattered by the cruelty of my peers. Most of the time, I would go downtown to City Center Mall and wander around for hours or go to friend's houses when their parents went off to work. Amazingly, while I missed school, I still made stellar grades. Even though I felt jaded on the inside, nothing would ever stop me from being a scholar. I remember coming home from school, crying about it, writing about it in my journal, and wishing that it would be over.

Eventually, I found refuge in the place that I would never imagine I would find – writing rap lyrics. While my mom did not allow me to listen to hardcore rappers like Lil' Kim, Trina, Jay-Z, or Juvenile, I became a fan after listening to popular songs on Power 107.5 during the bus ride to and from school. Our local library had a robust collection of rap CDs and I would check them out and secretly rip all the music on our home computer. I would turn the music on low when my family was home or blare it out loud when I was the only one there. Eventually, I began to write my own lyrics after listening to female rappers like Eve and Missy Elliot. Their "Me Against the World" attitudes and catchy lyrics empowered me to be as transparent, independent, and cool as they were. Writing raps made me feel strong and powerful. The cocky and self-assured nature of the artists in the early 2000s convinced me that I too, could have that type of freedom. From ages 12-20, I kept a rap book full of lyrics. Some lyrics depicted my life; others depicted a fantasy lifestyle I thought I might want to live one day.

As I write this book, I looked through an old scrapbook I created in high school, reflecting on my middle school experience with my haters and bullies for a junior year project in my English class. I found the lyrics scribbled on pink construction paper that read:

"I got haters on top of haters,
Call it a double-effect,
Used to get to me hard,
Was an emotional wreck,
Try to use a scary tactic,
Put no fear in my chest,
Started rumors about sh**
I ain't even done yet!"

There was more where that came from. Outside of journaling, writing raps became my therapy. I love the HBO show *Insecure* by Issa Rae because it reminds me of when I used to say my raps out loud, confident, and unapologetically, sometimes in front of the mirror, too! For a long time, I would say them to myself, but eventually, I let others into my passion project. When people learned that I could rap, they were always taken back. This four-eyed, skinny girl, had bars? It was almost like they were seeing a unicorn for the first time. But I was a unicorn. A unicorn with bars. Rapping gave me a sense of identity that I never knew that I had permission to have. I allowed my peers, television, and a low regard for myself control my dopeness. When I rapped, I temporarily evolved into a lady MC with prowess who controlled her own life, at least for sixteen bars.

Middle school eventually came and went. By the eighth grade, I realized that while I barely survived middle school, I had to woman up and understand that I had my whole life ahead of me to continue surviving. Middle school may have been over, but the rose of life, thorns and all, continued to bloom. I was beginning to be okay with that. Whether I looked like Buffy the Body or the bottom of someone's shoe, I could not control what people said or thought about me. I learned that I always had to be me, whether people liked it or not. At times, this is easier said than done, but as I have gotten older, I have learned to care less and live more. Why? Simply put, you don't need permission from anyone to tell you who you are or what you are worth.

I can't express enough that this book is so much more than just freedom. It's about a self-definition. When you define who you are, no one can take that distinction away from you. If you don't define who you are, you open yourself to living your life inside a box that was built by someone else's definition of you.

For most of my teens, I wandered aimlessly through life with no values. Don't get me wrong; my parents did their best to instill values into me. I was always polite, respected adults (for the most part), took my education seriously, stayed out of fights, went to the Kingdom Hall with my mom, and learned how to stretch my allowance money from here to Timbuktu.

But, there were some lessons that I missed. My mom never really talked much to me about boys. It was a conversation I think she honestly avoided because she thought her sternness and disciplinary attitude would convey the message to stay away from them. My dad was totally opposite. He first told me when I was eleven-years-old that all boys wanted was sex. And, if I was bold enough to get into a relationship, I should play the boy before he played me so that I didn't look stupid. I had a lot of mixed messages when it came to boys. I relied heavily on my friends, and, it was literally the blind leading the blind. We all were young, inexperienced, and based our relationship advice on things we saw on television and movies. I never knew what boundaries to have in place when dating someone. And technically, by both of my parents' standards, I wasn't allowed to date, so when I did have "situationships" with people, I had no adult in my corner I could be open with the share my concerns.

This hurt me in the long run. When I did become sexually active, at the age of fourteen, I contracted an STD. Three to be exact: gonorrhea, chlamydia, and trichomoniasis. I was nearing the end of the eighth grade and was still on a continued path of skipping school occasionally. This time it was for a guy, who I was head-over-heels with, even more so than the year before. He was also older, attractive, and a sweet talker. I lost my virginity to him and we had unprotected sex several times after that. He eventually stopped returning my phone calls, and I got the message that I was no longer wanted.

Later, I felt my body change. Sometime wasn't right. I casually mentioned to my mom that I thought that I had a yeast infection and she purchased the suppository at the drugstore and gave me instructions on how to use it. My symptoms subsided for a while, but a few days after I took it, I felt an inflammation. I knew I had contracted an STD.

For several months, I quietly burned in pain. I didn't know what to do. I was scared to death to tell my parents but I was even more scared of what I had. What if it was AIDS? What if I was dying? My best friend Annie knew about my symptoms, and she would encourage me to tell or go to the doctor. I eventually got over the fear of what the problem could be, but I didn't get over the fear of telling my parents. Until this day, they still don't know about it.

I put my Internet skills to use and did research on clinics in Columbus. I found a Planned Parenthood on the west side of town and took the #10 COTA bus to get there. The clinic provided services on a sliding scale and luckily, I qualified to get seen and treated for free.

The doctor was a nice, quirky, Caucasian woman who tried to make me feel comfortable. She asked a ton of personal questions, and I was so nervous that I thought she would call my parents and they would come and end my life, right there, in the clinic. She diagnosed me with trichomoniasis the same day, but I had to wait several days to learn about the other two STDs I contracted. Luckily, all three were curable, but that experience scarred me forever.

I knew a lot about safe sex and birth control. The Internet was my best friend and I researched everything I wanted to know before I made the plunge to lose my virginity. All I know is I was told not to have sex, but being a rebel at heart, I had to try it anyway. There are so many times I wish I could go back and reevaluate my self-worth. I wasn't stupid. I knew what could happen to me: pregnancy, STDs, yet I allowed it to happen. I was so anxious, so thirsty, and desired so much to be wanted that, I gave someone permission to denigrate my innocence in exchange for temporarily feeling loved and beautiful.

This trend for love followed me throughout high school. You would have thought I learned my lesson the first time, but I kept going. I had a weird mindset. As much as I wanted to be in love, like any other teenage girl, at the same time, I thought boys were trouble. I would be a liar if I said I didn't hurt people. I hurt boys as much as they hurt me. Sometimes more. I put my dad's fatherly advice of playing other people before they played me into action. It wasn't right, and I realized that after I ruined a special relationship I had with someone. His name is Ray, and he was probably everything that I needed for a high school relationship at the time. The problem? I didn't want it. By the time we ended up with each other in the tenth grade, my mind was so far gone from fairy tales. I had my heart broken several more times, and I was out for blood. Unfortunately, Ray got caught in the crossfire. He was a gentle person, despite his humble beginnings. He respected girls, was always positive, and treated me like a queen. I remember one year, for homecoming, I wanted two dresses, and he convinced his mom to allow him to buy both for me. At that point, that was one of the nicest things I guy had ever done for me, and it was almost overwhelming.

He would always listen to me ramble about my crazy ideas, and we would talk on the phone for hours at night. He proudly displayed his affection for me in public despite me protesting. I wasn't there yet. I was so used to concealing my relationships with people, so being in public was fresh to me. Ray and I would make up to break up several times. Eventually, we went our separate ways in high school, but I know that he still cared for me. I cared for him, but I never felt like I was good enough for him. He was someone with a genuine heart, and at the time, I felt like I sabotaged something that could have truly been special.

After some time passed, I eventually began to talk to other guys. Senior year, Ray moved on and I went on Ohio Dominican for my dual enrollment program. I began to talk to a boy named Christian. Christian was new to our high school and was on the football team with Ray. He was charismatic and was a seemingly great guy on the outside. People liked him, girls crushed after him, and somehow, we ended up talking. I really liked Christian at one point. He was a breath of fresh air and was nearly as much as a gentleman that Ray was to me.

One October day in 2008, we went on a date to the movies to see *Jack and Miri Make a Porno*. Prior to our date, we had been talking for several weeks, and I noticed that Christian was a little controlling. I didn't say anything to him about it because I just accepted the idea that he was a little rough. When we were around each other, he would grab me aggressively, and say things here and there in an intimidating way. I dismissed it. He wasn't like that all the time, so I just kept rolling with the punches. I didn't tell Ray that we were talking, and Christian made it explicitly clear that he didn't want Ray to know we were talking. At that point, they had served on the football team together, and apparently that bonds you for life. Between my stories and what he heard at the school, it was clear that Ray and I had an unspoken bond that he didn't want to get between.

As we watched the movie, we laughed at funny parts. Christian had his arm around me and I was comfortable. He kissed me in the theater. It was warm and smooth. I felt my heart flutter slightly. I was definitely into him.

What he did next happened so quickly and suddenly. As Seth Rogen and Elizabeth Banks plotted on how to make money from a low-budget porno, I was forced to give Christian oral sex at the top row of the movies. He grabbed my neck, held it aggressively, and told me to do it. I was scared out of my mind. The sweet person I had gotten to know turned into this monster that I never wanted to face again.

After the movie, the sweet person returned. I was in shock. I didn't have much to say, and when I went home, I locked myself in my bedroom and cried. I called one of my good friends from high school, Jorden. I told Jorden what transpired that night, and she cried with me over the phone. I felt like trash. Thrown away. I had always heard about girls being forced to have sex or do sexual acts, and I never thought that I would be one of them.

Christian still tried to talk to me afterwards. I think he knew what he did was wrong, but I began to avoid him. It made it easier that I didn't attend my high school the last year of school, but nevertheless, the pain remained. I felt broken and less than the brilliant, bright, and beautiful young woman that I was.

Although Ray and I had stopped being in a relationship, we were still friends. I told him what happened with Christian, and he made it his duty to make sure it never happened again. He confronted Christian at school one day, and told him if he ever touched me again, he would have to answer to him. After that,

Christian never looked my way again. When I learned about what Ray did, it renewed a sense of worthiness in me. He valued me enough as a person to defend my honor and helped me get through that traumatic experience. Don't get me wrong, he was upset, but he never doubted me, and I will never, ever, forget that. Ray will probably never know that he helped save my confidence and what little self-dignity I had left.

That experience was a wake-up call. It was time to do something a little different. I slowed down on "being in a relationship" for a while and got focused. I was going to finish the dual enrollment program and go to college soon. I didn't need any more distractions.

Some people automatically know who they are, almost as soon as they are old enough to be conscious of the world around them. But for many of us, it takes a little more life experience, a little more push, and a little more encouragement to manifest into the person we are meant to be. Self-definition takes self-actualization. Being aware of what drives you will be the biggest investment you can make when you embrace the thought that there is a life bigger than the one you have currently been living.

For years, I relied on other people to accept me. Loving myself became lost in translation, and it took a long time to understand what my worth truly was. I always used to tell younger girls that if I put as much time and energy into developing myself and being more disciplined with my education instead of chasing boys, love, and everything in between, I would be astronomically more successful. But later on, I realized that I was unconsciously on a mission to do just that: grow. Each life experience that I've had only led me to being a better person. Some of the experiences came with baggage, but I eventually learned to remove that baggage from my existence.

To be free, you must be unafraid of finding yourself and being comfortable with what you unveil. A powerful person lies between the person you are and the person that is waiting for you to find them. Recognize what your self-limiting barriers are, and don't let them stop you from getting to the best version of yourself. Your challenges should not discourage you, your past does not own you, your environment does not warrant you to be a product, and your relationships with others do not validate your why. Only you can put a seal of approval on your truth but you must be willing to accept that your former and current circumstances are not a part of that narrative.

Early on, I felt like I did not have solid values, and as a result, placed myself in situations where I did not appreciate my own worth. I would say yes when I meant "no," and put the needs and wants of others before my own, which often left me feeling like something eventually had to give. With each experience, I've grown wiser and developed a set of non-negotiables to help guide my path in life and allow me to become more focused on what matters to me the most. A non-negotiable is a personal value or activity that is not open for discussion or negotiation. Sometimes we learn from our parents, experiences, or other external influences. Sometimes, we intrinsically know that what's for us, is for us. Over the years, there are a few things I've learned that I won't stand for:

Labels. Long before I knew myself or the potential who I could be, I allowed myself to be placed in a box by others. Things like status, title, and validation from others no longer move me because I am making moves to define myself. The less emphasis I give to labels, the more focus I place on giving myself a shot to truly become the best version of me.

Abuse of any kind. Whether it's physical, mental, or emotional abuse, I will not allow myself to be subjected to it.

Being silent. When issues have risen in my life, I was silent. I was always taught to be non-confrontational, and I think I misunderstood when I should speak and when I should be silent. I was quiet for a long time, and now if I see something, I say something. No matter what kind of result it will bring. Wrong is wrong, and I refuse to stay silent, because my silence is equally as wrong as an act itself.

Not being in a state of joy. Happiness is a key element to freedom. I noticed that when I am happy, I am more productive, balanced, and confident about the things I am passionate about. Before I would allow other's energies, personalities, words, and actions steal my happiness and become miserable in the process. I've learned that while I cannot control how others treat me, I can control my own actions. Being around negativity is not up for discussion and I refuse to be in a situation that forfeits my ability to smile. Granted, I know that I won't be happy-go-lucky one hundred percent of the time, but when I can, I will not tolerate people or situations that jeopardize my joy.

The biggest thing I've learned through all of this is that if you don't stand for something, you'll fall for anything. This applies to your career, relationships, faith, and anything that you consider the nucleus of your life. In retrospect, when others see that you don't respect yourself or have a strong sense of values or non-negotiables, they will attempt to destroy you. One way to control that narrative is to surround yourself with positive affirmations. Whether you create a vision board, buy a cute planner/journal with sayings, or write on Post-It notes all over your wall, what you say and feel about yourself greatly impacts how you operate in life with self-worth.

Therefore, I am going to say this, and only say it once with no filter. **I am worthy as f***. And so are you. Don't let anyone convince you otherwise.**

While all the stories in this book are true, some names and identifying details have been changed to protect the privacy of the people involved. It's a small world.

Chapter Four Reflection:

1. What labels have others projected on you throughout your life? Did you believe them?
2. Describe the non-negotiables that you cannot operate in life without. If you don't have any non-negotiables, you can download "We Don't Negotiate with Terrorist" workbook on skinnyblackgirlscode.com under the Resources section.
3. Has there ever been a time that you felt unworthy or "less than?" What made you feel this way? Do you still feel the same way?
4. What things you do need to eliminate that threaten your sense of joy?

Chapter Five:
Take Care

"You're going to need therapy after this, baby girl. Get some help."

I stood next to my boyfriend, with my head hung low as his father sat firmly in a chair, arms crossed, feet flat to the ground, directly in front us. It almost felt like his eyes burned through my soul as his silent disappointment filled up the small kitchen at his house.

Somehow, Tyree and I managed to find the courage to tell his father that we had just left the abortion clinic a few hours ago. I didn't want to tell him; in fact, I didn't want to say anything to anyone. Unfortunately, we told both sets of our parents I was pregnant, and they would have gotten highly suspicious if a baby had not appeared in nine months.

"Therapy," Mr. Benson continued, "will be good for you. You are going to need a lot of help after this."

I listened to Mr. Benson's words out of respect, but I wasn't really listening to what he was saying. Black people didn't do therapy. That was something for crazy people. I wasn't crazy. I had just made a bad mistake, or as I would admit later, a terrible choice.

May 22, 2009

In the years following my abortion, I never tried to hide it. I have always been transparent about my experience to those who mattered or cared. Many of my friends and family who went through the same experience tried to block it and erase it from their memory. I acknowledged it almost every single day because it is something that is a part of my history. My abortion does not define me; however, it represents a period of my life where I woke up and started to view the world and myself a little differently.

My feelings of self-worth and value were at an all-time low when it happened. I was with a 21-year-old college dropout who was still searching for his identity. He came from a broken home and had influences that would not allow him to truly thrive. He was constantly at a crossroad between being someone and being mediocre.

I was well on my way to being someone. That school year, I entered college a year early after being accepted into a program that allowed inner-city high school seniors to skip their senior year and have their first year of tuition completely covered. For once, it felt like my intelligence truly got me somewhere, but it came at a cost. I missed my friends from high school and constantly scrolled through Facebook, sad about the things I missed out on while I was in away. I attended a small, Catholic, liberal arts university that was predominately white. This was the first time in my school career where I was the minority, and the pressure was on. All my professors knew I was essentially one of 24 guinea pigs from Columbus City Schools, and I knew that I had to make an impression. I made mostly straight A's (there was a B or A- in there somewhere, but who's counting?), placed in an accelerated Spanish class where no English was spoken, invited to my professor's house for Thanksgiving, and received a set of George Orwell's greatest classics from my poli-sci professor. College became a breeze after a while. I just never stopped giving my best, despite my experience with Christian. I couldn't stop.

May 22, 2009 is a day that is permanently ingrained in my memory. I remember laying on the operation table with a million thoughts in my mind. My doctor was one of the first abortion doctors in Ohio according to a nurse who gave me the rundown of his accolades before the procedure. Apparently, he was very instrumental in getting abortion legalized in Ohio, at one point in his life, and I was assured it would be all over quickly. When the doctor entered the room, he was in good spirits. Nothing in his body language and voice indicated doubt; I could tell that he had done this many times before. He said a few words to me to make me feel comfortable and gave a warning that I might feel some pressure.

As he did his thing, he and the nurse conversed about what they were going to do over the weekend. Meanwhile, I was a wreck. Ironically, I began to pray to God right on that table. It didn't hit me what I was truly doing until I laid on the table. Tyree and I went back and forth about what we wanted to do for weeks. Some days he wanted the baby, and other days he was worried that parenthood would ruin his future "baseball career." Despite dropping out of school, he had plans to return and finish what he started.

I became depressed during this time. I found out I was pregnant in the middle of the night when I felt a shift in my body in early April of 2009. Even though I had never been pregnant before, it's like I instantly knew that there was a change in my body.

I called up a friend with a car around midnight and we went to the Wal-Mart where I worked part time. I worked the day shift, so I wasn't scared to buy a pregnancy test, because no one knew me on the third shift. As I sat on the stall praying, "please, please, please," probably the worst prayer in the history of prayers, with my eyes closed, I opened them to blue lines. My friend hopped over the stall and screamed. She had become a teen mother a few years earlier and she did not hesitate to tell me to abort my child.

"You don't want to go through the shit I'm going through, girl," she said as she pulled up into the driveway of my mother's house. I nodded my head. I knew her struggles. I wouldn't make it as a mother. I wasn't strong. I was weak. I was still trying to figure out myself, let alone try to learn the ropes of motherhood.

When I told Tyree about our pregnancy, he was shocked, but he didn't dismiss my feelings. I think parts of him were excited, but like me, he had things he desired to experience in life that he had not yet reached. At first, we thought about being together, even toyed with the idea of marriage. Realistically, he and I were nowhere ready for that.

We met at Envivo, a club that has since been shut down and renamed multiple times. I was 18, 'independent', and in love with the nightlife. While I could have some fun as a teen, I did not have nearly the amount of freedom that many of my friends had. I vowed that when I turned eighteen, I would go out every weekend and engage in the fast lifestyle that I thought was for me.

He approached me, shining the most beautiful smile I had ever seen in my life. Unlike most guys I have interacted with in a club setting, he was respectful. He offered me a drink and we talked most of the night. We exchanged numbers, and I felt almost like I was on Cloud Nine. I was wary of guys after Christian, but something about him felt different. He felt like someone who was going to change my life.

For the next few days, we called and texted each other throughout the day. A week after we met, he invited me to his sister's birthday gathering at her apartment. He picked me up in his 2001 red Jeep Cherokee and held my hand as we drove to her place. When we got there, his mother and sister gushed at me as he held me close to him. When people asked him, he called me his girl.

I was a little taken aback at first. We had already known each other for a week, but it felt like a lifetime. Later, he asked me if him calling me his girlfriend made me uncomfortable. I asked him, what "this" was and he told me that everything he said at his sister's apartment was what he wanted. As crazy as it sounded, I wanted it, too.

Tyree and I were drawn to each other in a toxic and magnetic way. We both were obsessed and slightly possessive of each other. We spent nearly every day with each other, constantly on the phone when we weren't in each other's presence. I lessened my nightlife activities and focused on building with him. My friends didn't understand it. They saw something in him that I never saw coming. By the time I saw it, it was too late -- we were bonded for life.

After I announced that we would be parents, our relationship shifted. He began to criticize me and accuse of cheating on him. He knew that I had self-esteem problems with my weight and began to call me "fat" and talk about how ugly I would get when I grew in pregnancy. I started eating less, because I believed him. He got in my head in ways I had never experienced with any relationship before. He knew how to press my buttons.

In the midst of it all, I told my parents. Well, I told my dad, and he told my mom. They were hurt. Of all the kids they had together, I was the one that somehow messed up. My parents managed to raise three other daughters and a son with no teen pregnancies. I was supposed to follow their footsteps. My dad supported any decision I wanted to make, but my mom told me that I could "kiss a college education in Atlanta goodbye". Clark-Atlanta University, an HBCU in Atlanta, was my dream school. I think in her heart she wanted me to keep my baby, even though I knew it would hurt her to see me struggle. She would slide Watchtowers from the Kingdom Hall under my door each day, and I would sit in my room, confused and not sure of what to do.

Ironically, one of my childhood friends was also facing a similar situation. Jessica and I got pregnant around the same time, and we both debated about the pros and cons of getting an abortion. We were both dealing with young men who were unreliable and not ready to commit in ways that we needed to grow. We talked and decided that we would both scrounge up the money and do it together.

On the morning of May 22, all four of us went to the clinic. The guys were silent as Jessica and I went to the counter to check in. Jessica went first.

As I sat in the clinic, I looked around the room. So many women were there that day, and I could tell that all walks of life were represented in those cold leather waiting chairs. I tried to imagine what each of the woman's story was like, wondering if their boyfriends, husbands, and sex partners knew what they were doing at that moment. As I was lost in thought, I heard my name.

"White" the nurse called, as she read from a clipboard. I turned to Tyree and looked at him. He nodded his head and touched my hand. I pulled away slowly and walked towards the door. This was it.

I was instructed to take off my pants, cover up, and lay on the table. During my last few moments of pregnancy, I asked God to let me die on the table. Guilt filled my soul and I felt helpless. Every so often, I have a reoccurring dream that I slide off the table holding my stomach, saying, "no" over and over, in a white gown. In the dream, I walk out the abortion clinic, past protesters, and walk towards a light.

But I copped out. I didn't get up and walk away, like the dream I had for so many years afterwards. I stayed, believing that this was destiny and that I would get through it no matter what.

For years after that, that's what I kept telling myself. I convinced myself that I didn't need help and the only thing I needed was time to heal. Women got abortions every day. No big deal...right?

I was a damn fool. Time can never be a substitute for authentic repentance. I tricked myself into believing that I didn't need help and that everything would be fine. From the second I laid on that operating table on May 22, 2009, intuitively, I knew my life would never be the same.

So now, years later, the words of Mr. Benson echo through my mind. When I went through trials in my life, I realize that I refused to be self-aware. I was in denial about my feelings and opted out of confronting them. I sought refuge in time and believed that enough of it would produce results of healing. Instead of taking care of my mental health, I allowed it to collect residue from my past.

For years, I would cry for what seemed like no reason and have irrational mood swings. I couldn't stand the sound of a vacuum cleaner and I would cringe or close my eyes when people talked about or showed an abortion on television. For weeks, I couldn't sleep, partially afraid of the nightmares that I would have. One nightmare was me opening the door to a basement and seeing a floor full of dead babies covered in blood. Those dreams made me jittery and anxious; I was nearly never any good to anyone or myself the day following those nightmares. Panic attacks were a part of my normal routine, and one time, I contemplated suicide. I remember, a few weeks before going to Wilberforce, I stared at a bottle of pills at home. I wondered how many pills were in the bottle and how many it would take to put me to sleep so that I would never be interrupted. I never had the audacity to attempt suicide, but it would be a disservice to not say that it never crossed my mind. Black women have this "unspoken duty" of being resilient, strong, and unbreakable, but behind closed doors, we can be a mess. My life was living proof of messiness and the thoughts of suicide were unfortunately a dark part of my narrative. God has kept me through trying times, and I praise him for not allowing my disobedience and rebellious spirit further complicate my life, or worse, not allow me to have a life to live.

As time goes on, I realize that there is so much to live for. I have so many things to experience and grow from, and I get excited when I think about the opportunities in front of me and other women who desire to achieve freedom. One thing is for sure -- a big part of freedom is taking care of your mental health. When we are hurt, confused, or in shock from certain experiences, we can never truly move forward. Mental health is a branch of self-care and I had to learn the hard way to make it a priority. I've been down the road of not being able to get out of bed or not leaving my house because I was mentally, emotionally, and physically depleted.

I heard a TEDx talk that changed how I looked at my mental health. The speaker said, "When we get hurt or don't feel good, what do we do? We go to the doctor. Why don't we treat our mental health the same?"

I changed my view of mental health after hearing that talk. My peace of mind is valuable and I can't risk not having it intact. One of the most freeing moments I've had this year is acknowledging that Mr. Benson was right; I did need help. No, correction, I do need help, and that's okay. I am stronger than who I used to be, but I recognize the benefit and need to talk to someone with a professional background in helping people cope and get through their past. In the black community, we often speak about "praying" our way through problems. I believe in the power of prayer, but I also believe that God didn't put therapists and psychologists in this world to twiddle their fingers.

Knowing the next step in my mental health journey is one of the most freeing and satisfying feelings in the world. I recognize that healing is not always an individual process; it may take the interdependency of you, God, a licensed professional and your support system.

I attempted to talk to my parents about many of my thoughts, but the right words never came out. One day, I did try to tell them that therapy may be on my radar, but they didn't listen. My mother was worried that they would try to put me on anti-depressants and make me dependent. My dad told me I need to just deal with my feelings – as he has done for many years without outside assistance. I don't blame them for not supporting the idea of it, initially. I've kept my parents in the dark about many elements of my life, so they would never truly know the extent of the damage caused by my insecurities and decisions. I am no longer fearful or afraid to share my realities and I hope that one day, they embrace therapy as a necessary intervention to freedom for me.

I've learned how to cope with and focus on self-care and mental health throughout the years. One of the biggest lessons learned was becoming self-aware and getting out of my own way. Eventually, you will learn the value of getting out of your own way, too.

Sometimes, the biggest barriers we face in life are within ourselves, and they have nothing to do with our environment. It is a relief to place blame on "they." You know, the people and things that "stop" us from reaching our full potential of freedom and happiness. I stopped "not" taking accountability about my actions and attitude a long time ago, because I realized that "they" were sometimes a fixation of my imagination. I wanted an excuse not to be my best. I was fearful of what being whole would feel like again, so I accepted being broken and blaming others for the pieces that cut me deep. Blaming other people for the moves you have the capability to make will never manifest in the outcome you truly desire. You must do more than "embrace" being uncomfortable with your past, enemies, or current circumstances. You must RELISH in that sh*t and enjoy challenges along the way. They build you to become the best version of you.

I know where I've been and it pains me to see people, especially women, who believe that they can never get over the trauma that haunts them. For a long time, I spoke that depressing narrative in my life, often becoming overwhelmed with emotion when I mustered up the courage to look forward. Years after my abortion, I found out that Tyree had gotten married and had fathered two children with his wife. The first time I learned the news, I felt sick to my stomach. Here I was heartbroken and empty, and the one I fixated all my negative energy against was living life. He had moved on. I'm not saying that he didn't lose sleep, but somehow, he found the ability to move forward in his life. Why couldn't I do the same?

It took time, but eventually I learned that I was stronger than I gave myself credit for after doing these things:

Compartmentalize, but realize that you will have to face reality sooner or later.

Compartmentalization is defined as an unconscious psychological defense mechanism used to avoid the mental discomfort and anxiety caused by a person's having conflicting values, cognitions, emotions, and beliefs within themselves. I first began to compartmentalize after being sexually assaulted, and then began doing it full throttle, after my abortion.

As I mentioned before, I first learned about this term when I was undergoing business coaching for my first business. My coach told me that I needed to "compartmentalize" and learn how to separate my personal life from my business. While I appreciated her advice, it dawned on me that I had been compartmentalizing since I was 17-years-old. I placed all my unaddressed emotions in a compartment with the intention of never thinking about them again.

How? I focused on being a busy body. My mission was to become so busy that it was nearly impossible for me sit down. Being busy was my coping mechanism. If I was busy and constantly around people, I wouldn't have to think about the things that would keep me up at night. As I compartmentalized, I lost track of my actions. I indulged in things that I thought would bring me comfort, but instead those very things brought me more pain.

Now, nearly ten years later, here I am, opening that box. When I first began thinking about writing this book, I questioned how transparent I wanted to be.

Do I really want the world to know things that I've done and things that have happened to me? What will people say? What will they think?

Later, I realized that it didn't matter. Writing this book has been one of the most therapeutic coping methods of my life. I had to become "present" in unconscious thoughts; sometimes avoidance can indirectly lead to self-destruction or self-sabotage and my past reflect this sentiment. I had to re-explore my past with the mindset not to blame others or throw a pity party, but to search for lessons learned. I've dealt with so many things -- colorism, body image, bullying, abortion, sexual assault, and depression and I know that I am not alone in my trials. I truly believe that freedom exists within your own truth, and you cannot be ashamed or afraid to face those realities that you've survived. But first, we must slow down and acknowledge that such realities even exist.

Being busy is not a substitute for healing. It may feel good to be on the move and be a part of everything under the sun, but remember, these things are temporary. The sooner you give yourself time to heal from your past, the sooner you can focus on your present and future in confidence and good faith.

Learn how to be okay with the person staring at you in the mirror.

For a period of my life, it was hard for me to look back at the person in the mirror. At first, I struggled with my body image, and later, I could not bear to think about mistakes I've made in the past. I've beaten myself up over the years, and felt obligated to overcompensate for my sins by committing to doing good for others. As a result, I allowed people to walk over me, take advantage of me, and speak to me in ways that any respectable person would not dare to allow someone else to do in most of my adult life. "No" became a fantasy word, and I was eager to say "yes" and please others for the sake of "outweighing" whatever negativity I enacted or engaged in during my life. Later, I realized, I was hurting my self-esteem more than I was helping it. I stopped and backed away from others. I stopped volunteering myself for things and I focused on getting my mind on track. In that time, I learned that for me to have healthy relationships with family, friends, and coworkers, I needed to be secure within myself. I had to learn how to accept my truths, and be okay with them. I cannot change the past, which is inevitable; however, I realize that I have control of my present and future – it's all in my attitude. When I changed how I looked at life, it became easier for me to look at myself. I am a perfectly imperfect being and I am fine with never achieving perfection.

For most of my life, I've been taught to operate from a place of excellence. Naively, I believed that excellence equals perfection in all facets of life. Now that I've lived a little, I believe that thought to be untrue. Excellence is operating from a place of awareness. Knowing your strengths, capabilities, and areas of improvement will allow you to move forward. Excellence is a continuous cycle of desired development by understanding that you should not be stagnant in where you are but should always seek growth. Excellence is a lifestyle. The most brilliant minds in the world are not perfect; they operate from a place of being vulnerable and understanding that mistakes are necessary to find yourself. Build an unstoppable perseverance to push through and give life to everything in your power. When I realized that my power lies in accepting and acknowledging my truths, the woman in the mirror did not seem so distant. Instead of seeing where I was, I began to see where I am going.

Realize that showing vulnerability to others is not a weakness, but a necessity to take steps toward freedom.

I've worn a mask in my life for a long time. Friends, colleagues, and people who have read my blog have praised me on being so bold and confident. While I was being a champion for others, I never championed for myself. At least, until about a year and a half ago. I once believed that being vulnerable led to outcomes in my life, and if I hardened up and was less soft in my approach to life, I would be able to protect myself. While I hid myself from the world, I could not hide myself from my feelings. I began to question why I was so bitter on the inside and decided to do something about it. The first thing I did was to begin talking to my loved ones. One of the most important things I've discovered is that we cannot be afraid to share intimate thoughts, no matter how terrifying they are, with our loved ones. I often would get frustrated because it felt like no one was praying for me. Kendrick Lamar summed it up best in his song, "Feel" when he said, *"Ain't nobody praying for me."* I felt a raw emotion of loneliness from a lack of communication, or a stubbornness not to communicate what I've been through with those who needed to know. To heal, talk to people you love. They can't pray for you if they don't know what storms are in your life.

Figure out your happy space.

Writing has inevitably been a source of refuge for me, even when I was a young girl. When I was unable to verbally share my thoughts, I carefully tucked them away in a journal. Through writing, I have learned to express myself to the full extent of my capabilities. Later, when I started the Skinny Black Girl's Code, I realized that my words had the ability to reach and heal others. Women of all sizes have reached out to me to discuss how my blog has impacted their lives, often sharing their experiences, good and bad, with me. As I began to get to know more of my readers and their stories, it became clear to me that it was time to share my own.

Despite the storms in your life, find a happy outlet and hold on to it. This should be a medium that empowers you and sends you into an unmatched state of bliss. This is very important as you start to unravel your feelings and make the decision to move forward in your life towards freedom. Your happy place is your safe place, and no matter what it is, you can always depend on it to make you feel anew, but don't mistake a happy space with your personal redemption. Use that space to become inspired, but do not neglect getting help from family, friends, or a licensed professional. Freedom requires giving yourself permission to heal and sometimes that healing will require the help of others.

Chapter Five Reflection:
1. How will you commit to taking care of your mental health?
2. How will you allow others to help you heal?
3. What mediums can help you express your pain?

Chapter Six:
Love is Patient

On September 11, 2014, I sat patiently on a wooden bench in a slightly crowded, air-conditioned lobby of a courtroom next to my fiancé Jerome. I watched Jerome twiddle his fingers nervously as we waited to appear before a judge. We had been engaged since our sophomore year of college, and finally had the nerve to, you know, do it. After years of fantasizing about the perfect wedding, Googling the perfect dress, and thinking about the perfect songs to dance to at our reception, we decided none of that mattered. Or at least, I should say, I decided that none of that mattered. He would be happy either way. In the time that Jerome and I had known each other, we had faced the most unfathomable relationship turmoil, yet we lived and experienced the most magical of moments of our adult lives together.

"Barkley" the Bailiff called out. It was time for us to go in. Jerome and I looked at one another, locked in a gaze of fear and confidence all fused into one, we understood the emotion between us. We both stood up and walked in the courtroom, prepared for the destiny that was waiting for us on the other side.

I wish I could say that day was amazing. Perhaps, even arguably note that it could have been one of the best days of my life. But traffic court is a MOTHER. Ugh. Let me explain.

A week prior to our court venture, Jerome was pulled over in Gahanna, a small suburb of Columbus after stopping through town to say hello to my mother. He has just returned from a two-week trip to Philadelphia, his hometown, and was ready to get back to our small apartment in Cincinnati. A month prior,

Jerome was pulled over for failing to use a signal in Cincinnati and forgot to put an updated copy of his insurance in the car. The officer told Jerome to send in proof of insurance in and he did -- we didn't play that. I made sure of it.

When we were in college, Jerome was pulled over more times than the law should allow. Sometimes, I can totally believe it was his fault (he drives like a NASCAR driver); other times, it felt like he was a target. We a small minority in the middle of a cornfield and cow town in Ohio, so, I had my suspicions. Just to be sure, I convinced him to send his proof of insurance through mail and email. I even encouraged Jerome to call on speakerphone just to make sure it went through. The woman at the DMV assured him to go on to his trip to the City of Brotherly Love and everything would be taken care of from their end.

That's the last time I trust a DMV employee about to get off the clock.

What should have been a simple update in the system became a week of unnecessary complication. Of all the weeks Jerome could have gotten pulled over, he was slapped with a court date on what was supposed to be the most memorable day of our waking lives together. As I sat in the courtroom lobby that day, sulking, my mind traveled to the warning people gave us about getting married on September 11th:

"Oh my God, what are you all doing?"

"Um...do you not remember the bad things that happened on September 11th?"

103

"Why are ya'll being so extra?"

"Uh....I don't think that's a good idea, Whit. Can't you pick another date?"

I got the idea to get married on September 11 after conversing with an ex-coworker named Julia at a retirement party earlier that year. She and her husband got married on December 7, the date that will forever live in "infamy." In case you slept through history class, the Japanese bombed Pearl Harbor, a U.S. naval base in Hawaii, killing more than 2,000 people in 1941. While the date represented a tumultuous stain on American history, Julia's determination to get married regardless of what people said intrigued me. She and her husband eloped and were married for more than 20 years.

I wanted that kind of long-term commitment, and at that point, it didn't matter to me if we were married on Hitler's birthday. The date was only a small detail – at the time. Looking back, I think about the similarities of my could-be wedding date and the day it truly represents. September 11th was one of the worst days in American history. It is one of the few national tragedies that is permanently ingrained in my memory because I was old enough to pay attention, understand its impact, and witness its consequences, even today. While the rubble of the Twin Towers and the damages of the Pentagon have been removed and repaired, the day still leaves a light residue of shock in the country. The heinous acts of 9/11 eventually started the War on Terror, and for years, the media showed us pictures of men and women who risked it all to defend and honor America in name of justice and freedom.

Love is the same way, you know. At least, that's how it feels with Jerome and me. I would risk it all. I have risked it all. And I'd do it all again. Like war, love is evolutionary. It begins one way and gradually develops into a separation of winners and losers. The biggest difference is, unlike war, love is infinite, and will always produce victors and the defeated, over and over again. But victory is not solely awarded to a single individual who is bonded to his or mate with limitless devotion; rather, victory is awarded to those who operate as a unit and do not allow temporary defeats to reshape a mutual desired outcome of compassion, companionship, and commitment.

Now that I have been married for a few years, I often hear my friends, most of them single, talk about love. They often ask me, how did I snag a guy like Jerome, a man that never restricts my ambition, makes a mean breakfast, and holds my hand as we watch Netflix and chill. I often respond with a smile and say it was a strange twist of fate combined with a culmination of life experience and required growth from both of us.

When I was younger, I used to wonder how people stayed in seemingly perfect relationships. My parents separated at the age of seven and Jerome's parents never married, but dealt with each other for years before officially calling it quits. Therefore, my vision of relationship was highly influenced by movies like *Love and Basketball* or shows like *A Different World*. While each brought on conflict that left you wondering if reconciliation was ever possible, it was always comforting to know that a happy ending was always in sight.

Real life, to my dismay, didn't work like that. Relationships are work. They're hard work, but, it's worth it. When two people are willing to learn each other, accept each other's flaws, and make the choice to be happy, together, it can be a transformative feeling.

Willing. I want to backtrack to a seven-letter word that can carry a lifetime of meaning. I chose Jerome in 2010 after realizing it was time to do something different. I was bold back then. If I wanted someone, I would approach them -- I didn't have time for societal conventions. When I began to look his way, I was 19-years-old and a hot mess. I proudly brandished a T.H.U.G L.I.F.E tattoo, which stands for Truthful, Humble, Unique, and Genuine Life (it's always interesting to see people's faces when they see it) on my chest as I walked around my campus, performed in campus open mics with lyrics that would give Nicki Minaj a run for her money, and gave could care less about anyone or anything except myself and the education I was pursuing in college. In the midst of it all, Jerome was always around. During my freshman year, we had three classes together and he would often come and hang out in my room with my roommate to collaborate on music.

Jerome was different than most guys I've dated – he was quiet, stayed to himself, and was very disciplined. No parties, no alcohol, no smoking, no sex, no anything. Before Jerome came to college, he hadn't even been to a restaurant. His mother cooked meals all the time and he never wanted for a meal outside of his kitchen in life up until the age of 19.

His aurora intrigued me after getting to know him, but it did not hit me initially. Why? Because, like many women I meet, I was addicted to mediocre. When you engage in toxic or questionable relationships with others, either one of two things happen: 1) You become desensitized to being devalued and eventually accept mediocrity or pain as being normal or 2) You get tired of being tired and decide not to settle for the same ol' thing.

I've traveled down both paths, but for me, all roads eventually led to self-reflection and a lot of soul searching. I started to question whether my trend of dating the "crazies" was really a punishment from the Universe or a poor judgment call to sit down and really get to know myself before I tried to get to know someone else.

Looking back, I realize that I dealt with so many things in such a short time frame. Within a year, I had been sexually assaulted, had an abortion, graduated from high school and completed one year of college simultaneously, and moved to the middle of nowhere in Ohio to escape the humiliation, shame, and embarrassment I brought to my family. I never dealt with any of it. I just put all my attention on school, partying, or involving myself with guys to occupy my time.

While I wore a mask on the outside, I was dying on the inside and didn't know how to cope with it. For so long, being vulnerable was never an option for me. Being strong was an understatement. I lived with a mindset of being unbreakable, because feeling, hurting, and reflecting felt like signs of weakness. My panic attacks started to become a regular occurrence, likely caused by a mixture of school stress and built up emotions. Ironically, instead of gaining the infamous "Freshman 15," I began to lose weight. I lost my appetite for food, and honestly, for life. I went to Wilberforce to start over, but it felt like I was a hamster in a wheel, stagnated by a cycle of a familiar lifestyle that would not let me go off the course.

In the spring of 2010, I decided I had enough. I wanted to get back in control of my life; not just on the surface, but internally. I started to cut toxic relationships and began to get in tune with my feelings. I began to be a better person to those around me. I had suitemates in my dorm who never hesitated to "check me" on my reckless behavior. A first, I would argue and go to "Facebook War" with them, but over time, I realized that some of my flaws that they pointed out were worth addressing and working towards improvement.

As I began my transformation, I noticed Jerome every step of the way. He listened to my rants, only offering words when he thought they would be comforting or necessary. He was highly respectful and had the kind of presence that made me hesitate to curse around him at times, because I thought it would be offensive.

When I realized how much I liked him, I became nervous. All he knew was the crazy girl with THUG LIFE tattooed on her chest. In the time that he knew me, he never knew a vulnerable side of me. I wanted to show him the person I wanted and desired to become. Based on who he was, I felt like he would complement that growth, and eventually he did.

On April 21, 2010, Jerome and I sat in the laundry room at Henderson Hall at Wilberforce University and decided that we were going to be together, forever. Just like that. It was one of the most serious conversations I had in my life. Jerome had recently got out of a long-distance relationship and had the

108

mentality that if he was going to be with a girl, he wanted her to eventually become his wife. I had never met anyone my age with that mentality, and it excited me. *Me? A wife?* I was so hungry for change that I decided that I could think a little differently.

It wasn't easy in the beginning. Contrary to what others believe, Jerome and I had a rocky start in our relationship. Both of us will wholeheartedly admit that neither of us was perfect and we both did things that hurt each other intentionally and unintentionally. Regardless of our transgressions, we pushed through, and I think that is a concept that is difficult for most people to grasp.

Love is not rainbows and unicorns. It's sacrifice and hard work. It's mind-blowing. It's eye opening. It's everything that you can imagine and more – if you don't give up. I used to be the type of girl that would be ready to quit anytime that I had a problem in my relationship. There was always someone else that was a text away. *Shrug* After all, I grew up with the mentality that you play the guy before he plays you so I had no problem walking away if I felt like it was necessary. With Jerome, I had to learn how to reassess my mindset. No one is perfect, but when you find someone with a good heart and treats you well, you must learn how to humanize their mistakes. But it took work.

For months, I held onto a grudge that I had against Jerome. He had hurt me in the worst way possible. Although I forgave him, I couldn't let it go. Similarly, Jerome had animosity towards me as well – nobody said I was perfect. I became worried over time. Would we ever let it go? Was this it?

What seemed like the end became the beginning of something that we both needed: communication. Over the years, our communication style has improved immensely. We've grown from using our outdoor voices to allowing one another to speak and managing to go to bed with a resolution most of the time.

The biggest lesson I've learned from being in this relationship is that everything will never be the same. We've gotten older, our priorities have shifted, and we will never get back those years we spent together at Wilberforce University. Sometimes it is easy to hold on to old memories and allow them to dictate what you believe should always be your right now and your future. Do not allow old memories to overshadow the new memories that are capable of being created. Allow your life with someone else to manifest organically, and do not try to force something that is not desired by both partners.

The day after Jerome and I spent our morning at the BMV, we got married on September 12, 2014. Everything that could have gone wrong on our wedding day went wrong. His car broke down on I-71 South and we had to leave it in the parking lot of an outlet mall so we could get to our ceremony on time. As we drove in the car, Jerome started sobbing. I was alarmed - I didn't know if these were tears of joy or tears of regret. After I asked him what was wrong, he explained to me that he didn't feel like he was good enough for me. At that point, we had moved to Cincinnati, I had begun to quickly build my network and career, but Jerome was having a terrible time with employment and adjusting to a new place. He fell onto hard times when we lived together, and I often had to hustle so that we would survive with our expenses and bills.

When I heard him tell me those words of inadequacy, my mind immediately flashed to the very beginning of our relationship. It was a familiar feeling. I remember feeling like I was not good enough for him and thought that he would think that I was "damaged goods" given my past. I have always been an open book with Jerome in friendship and as a girlfriend, and eventually a wife. He was patient, has never judged me, and in that moment, I would not judge him.

"It's going to be alright, baby," I said, as I tried to comfort him. "We are in this together and we are going to figure this out."

He looked up at me and smiled. "Pretty lady," he said as he wiped his tears away. That was his nickname for me for years and his smile confirmed that he trusted me. Jerome is not a man of many words but his face told me everything I needed to know.

We got to Indian Mound Reserve near Xenia, Ohio and married next to a waterfall we visited as undergrads at Wilberforce to talk and dream about the future. My parents, aunt, and my professor and her beau attended the quick and intimate ceremony. While the day started terrible, it ended beautifully.

I was now Whitney Louise Barkley and that held a lot of responsibility. Being a wife was never something I had envisioned for my life, and I was, and still am, determined not to fail at it. It had taken a lot for me to get to that point and at the time of this writing. I am self-aware enough to know that I am nowhere near being the perfect wife, but I am better than the microwave dinner eating, workaholic, stressed girlfriend I used to be in the beginning.

An intimate relationship with a significant other is monumental. To experience real love is a gift, and it is one that is not devoid of sacrifice. As I look back on the "love locomotive" (he wrote me that in a letter once and it totally made my heart swoon) Jerome and I have ridden on over the last seven years, a few things come to mind to help you develop healthy and strong relationships that complement your journey to personal freedom:

Get to know yourself, interests, and values before taking on someone else's.

It is important to note that self-discovery and healing is a path to better, long-lasting relationships. Before Jerome and I became an official couple, I took several months to begin to reflect on who I was and who I wanted to become. I knew the life that I was living did not have a place in my future, and began to envision what kind of reputation, value, and honor I wanted to bring to my life. I started to become more selective of what I allowed to enter my world so that I could become a positive advocate for myself and be undistracted by the noise that had previously dictated my life. Because I had started attending church, I was on a path to forgiveness before Jerome was even in the picture as my boyfriend. These things were important to me because I did not want my past to prevent a manifestation of happiness for future relationships.

Looking back, I used to get in "situationships" with others because I was eager to take on their identity. I can recall dating someone for a time and taking on their way of talking, mannerisms, and ideals because I was void of creating those things for myself organically. As a result, I would often attract other "broken" men, because I had no substance of my own to offer them. My counterparts recognized this weakness and I would become heartbroken from the ways that they treated me. Oftentimes, I allowed their actions to define who I was instead of taking the time to create who I wanted to be.

Before you invest in a serious commitment, first, commit to yourself. Give yourself permission to have an identity that is reflective of you and what you believe in. Experience life in a way that challenges you to look at yourself in ways that you've never seen before. Take control of your thoughts, passions, and curiosity and allow them to mold you into a person with a backbone for truth. Your truth. Your current or future mate should appreciate your individuality and ultimately love you more because of it.

Invest a copy of Love Languages and take the test. You'll become more aware of how to give and reciprocate love.

The Five Love Languages: How to Express Heartfelt Commitment to Your Mate by Gary Chapman helped Jerome and I identify a critical needs gap in our relationship. In the latter part of our relationship, I felt starved of physical touch. The once playful, touchy-feely, man I once knew could go days without touching me and it drove me crazy. I began to worry and started to have negative thoughts about our relationship. In the same sense, Jerome also began to have worries. He would ask me to do things, often-simple things, like go to the movies with him or attend a comedy shows. I would often reject him, because I was too busy trying to build a career and brand in college and beyond. Jerome felt neglected, because the girl who once called him three times a day, was barely around and when she was, she was constantly glued to her phone or was interrupted by others who constantly needed her skills to build their brands.

I expressed my worries to a friend and she recommended that I take the Five Love Languages test online. I took the test and learned that Physical Touch was my love language. After much coaxing to Jerome, he took the test and learned that quality time was his love language. We read our results, but at the time, we did not know how to incorporate them. So we forgot about them, relying on our own inexperience and selfishness to guide the rest of our relationship. A year later, I decided to order the eBook, after being triggered by a video on Facebook that talked about the Love Languages. As I read, I started to bring Jerome in and we read the book together at night, often having a discussion at the end of the chapters.

Through our studies together we learned that our individual past experiences had a lot to do with how we treated one another. Jerome did not come from a family that showed love through physical touch, so he was perfectly fine without hugging and touching. But, while his family didn't have a physical touch relationship, quality time was most important to him. Jerome loves holidays and get-togethers that bring family together. He also enjoys exploring new places and things with the one that he loves.

I was totally opposite. My mother and father always hugged me every chance they had and I was also open to receive them. While they didn't live under the same household, my parents never stopped expressing their love to me through touch. Regular quality time with loved ones was never a priority for me because

I was the youngest in my house. My sisters and brother are older and had their own lives by the time I got to an age where I wanted a playmate. I have always been wrapped up in my own projects, since a young girl, and can easily lose track of time – even when I have plans with someone else.

Once Jerome and I identified our love languages and the root of our "why" for them, we began to understand each other more. Jerome makes an effort to touch and kiss me nearly every day and I have limited myself to the number of things I involve myself in so that I can spend more quality time with him. We do these things, not because they are expected, but because we love each other enough to do things that we wouldn't normally do for other people.

The Five Love Languages offer an opportunity for freedom because it allows you to introspective examine how you desire love. If you do not know how you want to be loved, it will be hard for someone to love you completely, if you cannot tell him or her what you truly desire. Everyday Jerome and I learn someone new about one another, but it is critical to have a foundation for your partner's love language because it can positively impact your communication, trust, and authenticity of your relationship.

Develop #RelationshipGoals that are beyond what you see on social media and mainstream media.

Like personal goals, you should establish regular goals in your relationships. The goals that I am referring to are more than just cute high definition Instagram photos with matching outfits 0n the horizon of the beach. I am talking about tangible and abstract goals you can evaluate over time. From the beginning, Jerome and I knew that we wanted to marry each other. It was a big declaration coming from a 19-year-old and 20-year-old who had barely scratched the surface of life, but we meant business when we said we wanted to be together forever. Because marriage was our goal, the way we dealt with each other was always intentional and cognizant of that goal. Long before Jerome was my husband, I learned to treat him with a level of love and respect I tried before. I challenged myself to look at our relationship differently and to operate in a way that was conducive for both of us.

At least twice a year, Jerome and I sit together and talk about our goals as individuals and our goals as a couple. We talk about what has worked, what has not worked, and what we would like to see from each other over time. We look at things like how we manage our finances, how we pray together, where we will travel together, and what things we can do to continue to make the communication in our relationship stronger than ever.

Over time, we've learned that we've had to make each a priority, because we are no longer girlfriend and boyfriend; we are husband and wife who operate as a unit. We make most major decisions together and learn how to respectfully agree and disagree with each other's views and opinions, because they will not always be the same.

One goal, in particular, is important to both of us: never abandoning who we are to please each other. It's important to understand that when you are in a relationship you will, without question, grow and evolve. Now growth and evolution do not always necessarily mean a 360-degree change; however, they are signs of progression from the person that you already are. The things that we require of each other to change are traits that can adversely affect our relationship (i.e. lack of communication), but we look to eliminate the bad trait and not the person. When you are in a relationship that does not allow you to be your true self, it will impact how you feel about yourself, which can ultimately cause regret, bitter feelings, and love lost.

If you or your partner feel like you've lost yourself in a relationship, set a goal to take time apart from one another. Spending time alone allows you to re-explore your identity freely, without pressures or expectations from your partner. Alone time is a critical element of self-care and it is needed to rejuvenate and restore yourself so you can truly be able to give 100% in your relationship.

Love is a beautiful thing. I am happy that I have found a man that loves me for me, regardless of what I've been through. Getting to know yourself is a lifelong endeavor and when you add another person to the mix, you begin to become introduced to parts of you that you may have never known existed.

Chapter Six Reflection

Personal freedom does not require a romantic relationship. But when you find yourself in love, make sure you are in a relationship that allows you to operate confidently as the person you are while promoting your continued growth. Remember to love from within through self-discovery and/or healing, so that you can adequately give and receive love to the special person in your life. *How will you make sure you are your best self for your partner?*

Chapter Seven:
Good Versus Better

I have a confession to make: I faked the Holy Ghost at church in front of at least 100 men, women, children, and a couple of pesky flies.

I admit I was wrong. Totally wrong. But at the time, I felt a ton of pressure to join follow the crowd. In 2011, Jerome and I used to visit an Apostolic church every Sunday while we were college students. Every week, someone was falling out of his or her seat, speaking in an unidentifiable language, and screaming as if his or her live depended on it. One of those Sundays, I felt something different. The pastor was giving a sermon about forgiveness and it touched me in ways I hadn't felt since I was baptized two years before. My usual calm demeanor led me out of my seat as I clapped and cried silently to the beat of the music and later on, his call to the alter. I almost felt like that day would be the day that I felt a transformative connection with God. Although tongues and catching "Holy Ghosts" were overwhelming to me at first, I admire the people who have those experiences. They have mastered showing their love for God out loud (literally and figuratively) and usually speak of experiencing an unmatched feeling of His love. When I saw it, I prayed to have one of those experiences, to show God, that I did, feel something for Him too.

Because I grew up in the Kingdom Hall, it was still pretty fresh for me to genuinely show my emotions in church. During the meeting (the Jehovah's Witness version of a church service) people were solemn and emotionless. The only time I saw people show emotion was when they clapped for something one of the

Brothers said about "Everlasting Life" or when new people were baptized during the Assembly, a huge convention of surrounding local congregations. Even during the songs, not much emotion was shown unless the song's theme required it.

As I cried and clapped, I wiped my eyes and noticed that friends from school, Jerome, and churchgoers were starting gather around me. All of a sudden it was like I was fresh meat, a freshman in the pews so to speak, as people surrounded and laid their hands on me. "

"Oh no," I thought to myself, as I slowly lost my focus on God and became conscious of the growing crowd around me. "They must want me to shout or fall out. I AM NOT ready for this!" As I was saying a silent prayer for them to find someone else to lay hands on and pray, the pastor began speaking in tongues. Then other people started speaking in tongues. Then I started speaking...something.

I think I said the same sentence over and over, but because it was so loud, I don't think anyone paid attention. The people around me rejoiced and prayed harder and I started shaking in my boots. Someone shouted that I was catching the Holy Ghost with a Hallelujah at the end of the sentence, but on the contrary, I was scared to death. I just wanted people to get away from me, but it seemed like no matter what I did, they drew closer. I was a Holy Ghost magnet for Pete's sake.

When it was over, people smiled at me and hugged me. I was mortified. Jerome said he was so proud of me but I hung my head in shame. Later on my friend Chalexis, asked me how it felt to catch the Holy Ghost and I admitted to her that I got nervous and just went with the flow so people would leave me alone. She burst out laughing and later on we both agreed that if I didn't go to Hell for anything else, that stunt would probably be my one-way ticket.

As I look back at that embarrassing moment, it is amazing to see how my faith has grown over time. Ten years ago, I couldn't tell you the first thing about a church, denomination, communion, or tithes. I'm still learning and growing in faith but I know that the presence of God in my life has been life-changing when I made it my mission to get to know Him, willingly and authentically. While I still have not had that tear-jerking moment of having God temporarily take over my body, I am secure enough in my faith to know that those moments aren't always defined by what we see in church. God has ways of getting through to us, sometimes in forms that are unexpected. For a large portion of my life, I spoke to God, although I never felt worthy of his presence or grace. I defined my worth by my mistakes and figured that any chance of redemption was crushed by my sins.

I was disobedient, partially because of ignorance, and partially because of my stubbornness to live life my own way. Earlier this year, I learned the phrase "obedience is better than sacrifice" and it intrigued me. I've always been aware of my rebellious spirit, and realized I was rebelling not only against, my parents, boyfriends, or the world: I was being disobedient to God. Although I began to make better decisions later on in my life and doing well, I was still being disobedient. How?

My curiosity led me to 1 Samuel 15:22. The verse reads,

"Does the Lord delight in burnt offerings and sacrifices as much as in obeying the Lord? To obey is better than sacrifice, and to heed is better than the fat of rams."

My "sacrifice" was overcompensating for my sins, by becoming a "do-gooder." I wanted so badly to outweigh the negative things in my life that I began to immerse myself with good things that would make me feel better about myself. I felt that if I did "good" I would balance out the wrongdoings I had committed.

With each action I felt temporary relief, but my guilty feelings never subdued. Despite doing good, I still wasn't giving God 100%. I was still not being obedient, because although I began to truly believe in him, I did not obey Him. Coupled with those feelings, I began to experience emotional burnout from trying to raise my moral bar so high and not allowing myself heal through God. No amount of good deeds will erase your past if you do not come to terms with it, accept what happened, happened, and confide and listen to God on how to move forward.

The idea of God was merely a convention that I did not integrate as the core of my life. I am ashamed to admit that for a long time, I knew God, but did not seek the will to have a true and meaningful relationship with him. God was a convenience when I wanted to do life my way. We are often convinced by sight and susceptibly insecure in our faith when life takes the reigns in a direction that was totally unplanned. I cried out to God when I had a problem or when I wanted something so bad that I knew that it would take more than myself to adequately make it happen. My relationship with Him wasn't reciprocal; all I did was take, take, take, and was too selfish to really give God the time and attention that he deserved.

"God, am I a good person?" I often pray. Some days I feel like a woman of virtue and other days I feel ashamed. The word "good" has several definitions. It can be used as a adjective, adverb, or noun. In particular, the noun reads, "that which is morally right; righteousness."

Righteousness. Such a long and powerful word. One word that I would find hard to describe myself at one point in my life.

Being good is not easy. Sometimes it feels unreachable. But it's possible – to have good moments. I have those instances where I feel like I have a clean slate to live another version of my life. A good version of my life. Sometimes when I strive to be good, I feel like I am striving to fail. Freewill can get the best of me and I am not afraid to admit it one bit. I've accepted my flaws and mistakes and try my best to avoid them.

Sometimes I win the battle of resisting and ignoring my demons and other times I am broken – but not defeated. I am better than I was yesterday, last week, last month, and last year. Each day brings an improvement. Would I say I am good? No. Would I say I am better? You better believe it. See, to be "better" is "to improve on or surpass (an existing or previous level or achievement)."

I know I can never be good. I have good tendencies. I have good values. I have a good heart (most of the time). But I don't always have a "good" conscious to make decisions that will allow me to proudly wear an invisible "good" sticker across my forehead. It is impossible to foresee and sometimes prevent the moments where "good" goes out of the window and you adversely drifted away from your character.

I believe that God knows my heart. He can read my intentions. He knows that I sometimes I do the very bare minimum and sometimes I give every last ounce of me to achieve a level of goodness that is pleasing to him and to those who matter most to me.

I say a different prayer now. I do not ask God if I am good, but if I am better. I always want to be more satisfied with the woman I see in the mirror today than when I saw her yesterday morning. I know there is good inside of me. Realistically, I know this "good" will not always transpire through my darkest moments, although I will give my all to push through them.

When you recognize who you are – who you really are – you come to terms with a lot of things. I am an imperfect human being covered in sin but made up of faith. Perfection is not my goal but bettering myself is mandatory for growth. I am working to become the best version of myself and if I know God like I think I do, that "good" is good enough.

It took me twenty-six years to realize that my journey did not have to be as rough if I was willing to find God and accept Him early on. Instead I took a detour on faith, using my own ignorance and inexperience as a GPS for living. Through my stubbornness, God led me to these lessons that I feel compelled to share to help anyone who may be struggling to solidify their relationship with God:

Freewill can lead to bad choices. Free will can also lead you to God.

I've had my share of mishaps. This book outlines some of the ones that have changed me – for the better. However, my redemption began when I became so disgusted with myself, my situation, my decisions, and felt conviction for first time. Conviction is the act of realizing your sins and repenting to move forward. Freewill led me to place accountability everyone else but on myself. I blamed my parents, the world, and God for the bad things that would happen to me, but in reality, I only had myself to blame. Once I felt conviction, I felt hungry for change. I wanted to do better; not just by overexerting myself with good deeds, but truly get to know God. Understand that God will allow you to sin to bring you back to him. It took me multiple attempts to get to Him, but now that I am aware of his power and presence, I begin to pray over my decisions. Before, I would do make a decision without thinking twice, but now, I consult with God to truly determine if I am making the right choice. If I come across a decision that I know I couldn't fix my lips to pray to God about, I quickly learn to eliminate it.

Get to know your intentions and determine if they are accordance with what God desires. If you are unsure of what God desires, make an uninterrupted effort to get to know what he desires for his children. It is so easy to place our wants and needs in front of Gods, but it is a necessary part of freedom to know WHO you pray to, WHAT He expects of you, and WHY you should be obedient and follow his Will. Transformation in your life starts with your will to know Him and without getting to know his word, insanity will ensue. The word insanity is used as admiration for the infamous quote, "Insanity: doing the same thing over and over again and expecting different results." When we consistently use our free will for our agenda, we will continuously yield heartbreak, confusion, depression, distrust, imposter syndrome, and other similar trials we face in our lives.

Understand that God does not give us trials to "end" us, the trials are to help us grow as individuals. When facing a trial, do not worry because it is leading you to a greater purpose. There have been trials in my life that I have failed, some of the same trials more than once. At times I could not overcome certain desires, but in my heart I knew I could do better.

Whether you realize it or not, your faith boils down to the values you have set place for your life. When I honestly reflect on my life, I did not have true values. I have been relying on being a "good person" while never truly embracing what that means from God's perspective. I've done bad things blatantly and thought that if I do good things it will balance out my sins. If you have encountered these feelings, explore seek God, so you can stand against your trials. Sometimes God's Will is as clear as day, and other times it may take some searching for understanding. Develop the will to develop strong values around God's Word and stick with them even when the trials in your life seem larger than life. When we place our trust in God, the impossible becomes possible. Nothing is too powerful for God, but you have to first believe and genuinely decide to seek him and his desires for you.

Hopelessness can feel infinite. But with dedication to your faith, struggle has an expiration date.

From the date of my abortion until the day I was baptized in church, I felt strong feelings of hopelessness. Nothing could make me feel like I had a life worth living. I knew God but what little obedience I had surrendered to the depths of my sins. Believing no longer felt like an option until I made church a more regular part of my life. Once I began to immerse myself, first in church, and then later through personal Bible study, I no longer felt like my life was a lost cause.

Remember those SMARTER Goals I mentioned in Chapter One? On the SMARTER Goals sheet, I have a section for "Spiritual Growth". My goals were to dedicate time to read a verse from the Bible every week and to transform my abortion story into a testimonial to help other women grow and know that they too can live life beyond that unimaginable pain. Reading verses from the Bible every day filled me with more conviction, and allowed me to be open to doing life a different way. God's way. As I began to learn and journal about some of the people in the Bible, I found courage and strength to write this book. The Skinny Black Girl's Guide to Freedom has always been my goal, but through God, it became clear that this book was more than what I initially envisioned it to be. I needed to share my story in ways I had never been exposed to before. I learned to be transparent with God about my thoughts, feelings, and fears, and he gave me the strength to be transparent with others.

Be dedicated in your efforts to read it and understand the Word of God. I recommend writing notes in a journal or dedicated place so that you can reflect and learn how to apply the Word to your life. Studying The Word allows you to become more confident in your faith and becomes a point of reference when new situations arise. I'm not saying that you have to read the Bible in a month, but when you make it a part of your schedule, you will see a difference in how you evaluate life.

Here is an example of how I journaled:

Hebrew 11:5-6

By faith Enoch was taken from this life, so that he did not experience death: "He could not be found, because God had taken him away."[a] For before he was taken, he was commended as one who pleased God. And without faith it is impossible to please God, because anyone who comes to him must believe that he exists and that he rewards those who earnestly seek him.

My Notes:

"I must continue to believe in God in order to please him. I must believe wholeheartedly that I will be rewarded with his grace and promises if I seek a lifestyle and belief in him. Enoch is an example of someone who believed with everything he had and God allowed him to "not" experience death. I am unsure if this is in a literal or figurative sense, but regardless God took care of him because of his unyielding belief in him."

Notice how I said, "unsure". When I began to take notes, I was scared of observing the wrong thing or not truly understanding it. I think that is why I ultimately avoided the Bible for a while. But, as you take notes, remember they can be as simple or complex as you like. You will not always understand what the Bible says, and it is good to consult with – just give yourself an opportunity to immerse yourself in God's words and allow them to become your personal GPS.

Remove distractions and listen to God. He always comes at the right time.

For my entire life, I have relied on my own understanding to make choices. I did not ask God to lead my choices; rather, I would simply just ask for his support. There are a lot of mistakes that could have been avoided in my life if I just listened or asked for help. Now that I am pursuing a straighter path in life, I know now it is critical to seek God and understand his word. I need him in my life and I want to ensure that my purpose is fulfilled through his Will. I realize the Enemy will attack me more through this process but I cannot allow that to slow me down or stop having faith in the power of God.

About two years ago, I had a friend in Cleveland who told me that she was waiting for God to "order her steps," as we sat in in her living room to celebrate her 25th birthday. My friend desired to go to law school, worked in a job she despised, and was working on owning her first car. As a highly ambitious go-getter, I could not understand what was taking her so long. There was financial aid, car loan options, and plenty of other jobs in Cleveland. What was the big deal? Selfishly, I thought, "If this was me, I would have been done these things already." But it wasn't me and I didn't humble myself to place myself in her shoes. I never truly understood what my friend's words meant until it was time for me to say the same thing, not even six months later.

You see, you cannot allow your own impatience and anxiety for something to happen to take precedence over patience and obedience. Through God, you will find the best clarity and direction you will ever need. But it starts with listening. In order to listen, you have to remove distractions from your life, or at the very least, remove yourself from your distractions. Distractions come in many forms: friends, relationships, family, jobs, social media, bad habits, life turmoil….the list can go on. Once you identify your distractions, you have to make an executive decision to no longer allow them to become distractions.

When I lived in Cincinnati, I felt stretched too thin and all over the place. I never had the opportunity to know what I wanted or what God wanted because I so involved, and so distracted with different things that promote my career. When my husband and I decided to relocate to Columbus, I gained so much clarity. Most of my childhood friends had moved out the state, I didn't have much of a professional network, and I didn't work in the city immediately. Moving to Columbus allowed me to reevaluate my priorities and reestablish my personal relationship with God without distractions. For the first few months, I was still. I asked God for help with my next steps and to not allow me to be hasty. God connected me with people in Columbus who had that same spirituals desire as mine and I learned to grow from their advice and presence.

Eventually, God began to speak to me. He told me to stop operating in my business the Barter Babes and told me to start working in my gift of graphic design and social media. He told me to cut relationships with people who brought me more harm than happiness, and told me to give more of myself to my husband. Then, one of the biggest revelations he gave me was to forgive Tyree. I hadn't thought about him in years, but, as a part of my SMARTER goals, I added forgiveness to my plan. Forgiveness included him.

I went to find his Facebook page and looked at it. I scrolled, looking at photos and statuses. The anger I once felt looking at him disappeared. I began to smile. I could no longer hate him. Hating him would not be reflective of the journey I had taken with God. Baggage from my past could not jeopardize what I've built with God.

In that moment, I prayed for him, his wife, and his daughters and wished Tyree a life of happiness and abundance. When I finished praying, felt like the chains from my past had been broken. I was free. I was in control of my life again.

It took the seeking of God to get to that moment. If I had tried to overcome my past by myself, I would still be filled with regret, hurt, and sadness. While I hadn't thought of Tyree in awhile, God knew that in order for me to find the clarity I needed, it started with forgiving him with my whole heart. But, it required asking God for clarity and actively listening for an answer. The Bible verse Proverbs 3:5-6, states, "Trust in the Lord with all your heart and lean not on your own understanding; in all your ways submit to him, and he will make your paths straight."

Trust God enough to know that he will give you the right answer at the right time. Allow patience and faith to keep you rooted in the belief that God is here for you, always.

Spiritual Affirmation

This is a spiritual affirmation that I have created to help guide me in faith. Feel free to use it or create your own based off of your own experiences with God.

"I must always take a chance on the good and keep the negatives to a minimum. While I can never be perfect, but I will always strive for a better me. No longer will I abuse myself or let others get inside of my mind, body, and spirit to destroy my confidence or freedom. From this day forward, I am creating a life that is inclusive of God and his Will.

God is my strength. When I felt like dying, he kept me alive. When it felt like the tears were never going to stop, he dried them up and gave me hope. He is a truly amazing force that is helping me in unimaginable ways."

There are going to be barriers along the way, but with confidence, love, and faith in God, I will walk through those barriers as if they were an open field.

Chapter Seven Reflection
Read the following scriptures and journal your thoughts:
- Proverbs 3:5-6
- James 1:2-3
- Hebrews 11:4-6
- 2 Corinthians 13:5-9
- Hebrews 11:32:40
- 1 Samuel 15:22
- James 1:6-8
- James 1:4-5

Chapter Eight:
Yet

Adrienne was one of the first friends I made when I moved to Cincinnati. We had a lot in common: we both were born and raised in Columbus, loved trap music, and were millennial, black, and female professionals navigating through our careers in the Queen City. We became acquainted when we mutually worked for a nonprofit that dedicated itself to provide a job readiness program for impoverished people through meaningful full-time employment. While I was a newbie employee in 2013, Adrienne was a well-respected and highly visible asset in our company. With a Master's Degree from of Cincinnati's best criminal justice programs and a strong track record in helping our employer's population of men and women remove legal barriers to find employment, Adrienne was on top of her game. She was efficient, dedicated, loyal, and...stagnant. While she loved the work she did and the people she served, there was a burning fire in her to do something else, something well beyond her comfort zone.

Every day, I would stop at her cubicle and chat with her. Sometimes we would talk about work, sometimes about music, but often, our dreams. As I sat in her cube, I noticed a yellow sticky note. On the note read the word, "yet." Out of curiosity, I asked Adrienne what the word meant, and she explained that "yet" was her reminder that the best was yet to come and she was patient in waiting for the next moments of her life. Within a few months of meeting Adrienne, her "yet" came true; she packed up her life in Cincinnati and moved to Florida to pursue a promising legal career within the government section. When she cleared out her desk, she left me her sticky note – she suggested one day that word would have value to me too. Adrienne was one of my biggest cheerleaders and always kept me motivated and confident at work while encouraging me to always follow my dreams outside of my 9-5. I was going to miss her. But what I valued the most about her was her unyielding belief that my "yet" would be soon to come. Until this day, I keep that sticky note, and as I close, I want to instill that belief in you, that your "yet" lives beyond your wildest imagination.

The word "yet" has three different meanings. The definition that I would like to focus on is what I believe is the most important for maintaining your freedom. Merriam Webster's Dictionary describes "yet" as "but at the same time; but nevertheless." The word "yet" is critical to the success of how you continue to find peace and confidence in freedom. Take this statement for example:

"I may not be perfect, yet I have found deliverance from my past and hope in what the future brings through personal freedom." That yet can be a powerful connector of your right now and what you desire in the future. Additionally, "yet" can help you see the bigger picture when obstacles prevent you from being able to clearly visualize the life you view for yourself.

Remember, personal freedom exceeds the outskirts of an internalized declaration; it is a lifelong commitment to getting to know yourself. It's easy to desire the satisfaction of detachment from crucial issues that have cast a shadow over your abilities to become your best self. Once you identify what freedom means to you, the journey to attain it feels like more than a goal – it becomes a mission.

After you experience autonomy for the first time, it is necessary to know that the "mission" is far from being completed. When you feel a sense of accomplishment, particularly when you overcome a barrier in your personal life, it is easy to convince yourself that you have made it and no extra actions are needed to maintain your feeling of victory. Whether you believe it or not, that moment you breathe life into that conviction, it the moment you lose the freedom you just worked so hard to attain. The word "yet" can become your savior in this instance because it is a reminder that in spite of adversity there is still room to move forward.

When I worked in the nonprofit sector, I helped formerly incarcerated men find employment, sometimes immediately after their release from prison through the job readiness program, I mentioned earlier. Many of the guys that I encountered in the program were hungry for a better lifestyle: they had just finished serving time and desired the freedom of going back into the world to reunite with family and friends, find gainful employment, or return to school to complete a diploma or start a GED program.

More often than not, they were positive and had a winner's mindset. They served their time, were changed men and were ready to do things right. Who wouldn't appreciate their transformation? Society, unfortunately. While the men felt a change within and were anxious to live the lifestyle of abundance they had planned for themselves, they were often rejected because of their criminal record or lack of a high school diploma. Their families and friends mocked their efforts and sustained adverse environments that threatened their self-confidence and intent to change. While being locked up gave these men a change of heart, the world beyond the prison walls would not allow them to separate themselves from the life they were trying to escape. As a result, I've seen many guys who go through the job readiness program, come to the facility each day and job search, and then slowly disappear. Because they believed they were "done" once they finished their time in prison, it became a reality check when life did not flow in their favor immediately. Later on, we would find out them the friendly and determined men we would see hammer out twenty job applications in a day on the news for committing a new crime or in the obituary. Despite their hiccups, several of the men continued to believe in a future for themselves, and I would often hear many statements with "yet":

"I may not have a job yet, but that doesn't mean that I am not good enough or can't get it done. It's a waiting game. I know something will come through."

"Just because I don't have a car yet, doesn't mean I can't make it to work. I'll find a way -- I'm ready to make money."

"I don't have it all together yet, but I am going to keep trying. Someone will give me a job."

Saying "yet" became a catalyst of hope for these men and was a large part keeping them on the path to a better life. On the flip side, many of them would come back to our program, and try again, but when they did, their motivation was different. While the men still had the desire to try again, they are scarred from the events that transpired during the first go-round. As a result, they experienced a shift in their mindset and self-doubt became a mentor barrier that became hard to overcome.

135

My experiences working with the latter of the men who could not overcome their rut taught me not to become comfortable with my "right now" feelings, because as you are well aware, life has a way of throwing curve balls, especially, when you are building a life on your terms.

It is fair to say that we often get caught up when adversity corners us in a difficult place. Personal freedom seems so hard to acquire, but the real journey starts when you work to preserve its presence in your life. You have to be constantly aware of your emotions, thoughts, words, and surroundings because it is easy to slip into a negative state of mind without realizing that you are slowly drifting away from your independence.

I never want to merely try to do my "best" at maintaining a life of freedom – I will give it my all. I say this with extreme confidence because there are days where I feel the opposite of revolutionary, transformed or any adjective that describes progress. I am learning that to continue a mindset of abundance, I must learn to sacrifice, believe in myself, and remain humble. I'm not perfect, and I strongly suspect I never will be. However, as long as I acknowledge and address my imperfections with better behaviors, better actions, and better intentions, personal freedom will always be in the palm of my hand.

But how do you get to this point?

I will admit, maintaining personal freedom can be a challenge. As easy as it is to tell someone to be positive, forgive yourself, forgive others, and make changes, it is challenging to repeat those actions every single day. Surrendering to negative emotions is relatively easy and requires little to no effort because you have felt those feelings before. As painful as they may seem, they are safe and comfortable. You know what to expect, the results are no surprise, and you have less pressure to remove yourself from that place of hurt. Freedom, however, can be intimidating to maintain daily. You may feel like you are undeserving or are making a mockery of yourself. You may feel overwhelmed because being strong and unbothered takes genuine effort.

My intention with this book is to be transparent and ultimately provide sound advice that lets you know while I have overcome many barriers in my life, I am still a work-in-progress who fights daily to become the best version of herself. I have had many victories, but I have not "arrived" to any final destination because I realized that freedom is perpetual motion and is not a journey's end. While I may not have all of the answers, I want to share some of the strategies that have kept me in this mindset to never give up on myself while continuing to create the best life for myself and those around me:

21/90 Rule

The 21/90 Rule is a philosophy that suggests that it takes 21 days to form a habit and 90 days to create a lifestyle. According to Dia T., author of Power of Habit: 99 Healthy Habits to Relieve Stress, Eat Healthy, Feel Good and Increase Energy, Tom Bartlow is the originator of this rule and identified three stages associated with someone who desires to create transformational habits within themselves and lifestyles:

The Honeymoon: The honeymoon phase describes the state of happiness you reach when you start a new habit. You are inspired by something that makes you believe that the process will be easy. For example, at my non-profit job, we would often bring in guest speakers who were members of our program. Sometimes we had rare success stories when formerly incarcerated men found employment within several weeks. Their stories would often inspire other men in the program and give them hope that they would also be able to earn gainful employment to support them and their families.

My Advice: Hold on to the optimism you feel in the Honeymoon phase in your journey to freedom. In the days ahead, you may face incredible adversity that will have you question yourself and your efforts. Treasure and store that optimism for a rainy day because when you face an obstacle, you will need that feeling of confirmation to help you remember why you started.

The Fight Thru:
Reality sets in during the Fight Thru stage. You are no longer inspired and begin to struggle with new habits. You start to feel tempted to go back to the old you because it is familiar. Continuing the example of my nonprofit clients, this is when the going gets tough. These are the weeks where they would spend weeks applying and interviewing and never seeing a result. In some cases, they could not understand why they were not employed, and others began to feel doomed because of their previous track record.

My Advice: Once you identify the changes you need to make in your life to achieve freedom, you have to be willing to sacrifice temporary relief to gain long-term rewards for your efforts. While it may be tempting to slide back into old routines and habits, you must declare that is not who you are. If you do slip up, don't beat yourself. We often tell ourselves a narrative that because we make mistakes, we are no longer worthy of the path we begin to create for ourselves. If old behaviors come your way, reflect on why you indulged in them. Identify where you could have done better and make a commitment to how you will move on. Progress is never short of setbacks, and you have to be willing to allow your comeback exceed your shortcomings.

Second Nature:

One of my favorite songs of all time is from the Disney film, The Princess and the Frog. The protagonist of the movie, Princess Tiana, sings a song called "Almost There."

Within the song, Tiana mentions her town of New Orleans being a distraction as she works to own a restaurant that served mouth-watering beignets. Ultimately, Tiana's song represents why the second nature phase is all about how you manage your distractions. Going back to my work experience, the men who job searched faced many distractions that ranged from their family to their ability to the lifestyle they were desperately trying to leave. While they had found their groove for getting back on track, the simplest distraction could eliminate all of the progress that they had just experienced.

My Advice: Get to know your distractions. When you are building a habit, it takes great discipline and sacrifice to achieve your goal. If you are oblivious to your distractions, it will feel like you are in a hamster wheel, constantly going in circles.

Know what is in your way do everything in your power to eliminate it. Sometimes, the removal of a distraction means removing yourself from certain circumstances.

I am a believer of the 21/90 Rule and have felt all three of the phases that Tom Barlow defined. I've used this rule for prayer, healthier eating, and eliminating toxic relationships in my life. The only way that this rule can truly be transformational is when you permit yourself to be deserving of a life that allows you to feel free.

Find Accountability

The American Society of Training and Development (ASTD) conducted a study that found that 95% of goals can be accomplished when you regularly check in with an accountability partner. An accountability partner is someone who keeps you focused on your endeavors and calls you out on your B.S. when you are not doing what you are supposed to do.

In the last two years, I have found success in my life by surrounding myself with accountability partners. Notice the "s" in partners. I look for other people who are aligned with the different goals for myself and have them keep me accountable in that facet of my life. For example, I have a spiritual accountability partner who helps me navigate through faith and helps me regularly pray while I have a business accountability partner who helps me follow through with my business goals. Earlier in 2017, I took a step and held a mastermind group with three other women. Each Wednesday at 5:00 am, we would have a conference call from New York, Ohio, and North Carolina to talk about how we could improve our habits to increase profitability in our business. We met for about three months, and I am proud to say that each one of us has accomplished significant things in our business during the subsequent months.

When I look back, my nonprofit work was my first teacher of real accountability in adulthood. When I first began working, I started as an AmeriCorps job-search assistant, helping our clients on the computer and filling out applications. Later on, I was promoted to a full-time employment coach with the organization. As a coach, I was responsible for keeping my clients accountable. I had to dig deep to understand their barriers and help them come up with solutions to overcome the obstacles that prevented them from obtaining employment. Sometimes my clients would have excuses and other times they were depleted of motivation. In my personal life, I was also facing some of the same realities, but working with my clients and working through their problems, helped me with accountability for myself. I felt like I could not help others unless I was also trying to achieve a better me, and that is exactly what I did. My clients would never know this but helping them helped me in ways that I never knew would happen.

If you are without an accountability partner, I suggest aligning yourself with people who are like-minded and desire to see you succeed almost as much as you want to see yourself succeed. When creating a relationship for accountability, set regular check-in days, because the consistency of meeting will encourage you to move on your goals and not be stagnant. It is essential to also set a timeline for your relationship. How long will you work together? Six weeks? Three months? A year? A serious accountability relationship should require a timeline to make sure that all partners are respectful of each other's time.

If you are without an accountability partner, consider finding a mentor. I have been fortunate enough to have many mentors in my adult life who have given me advice in both business and my personal life. When you seek a mentor, it should be someone who you admire and has already achieved a level of freedom that you desire. When you find a mentor, be sure to understand how you can complement their life, because after all many dedicate time to talk to you and challenge you to become better for free. Alternatively, another important way to find accountability, believe it or not, is becoming a mentor. When you reach a peace of mind, mentor someone who may be in a place that you've experienced in your life. As your mentee reveals their truths to you, it will help you expose your insecurities. You might find that the advice you give them, might be the same advice you should take for yourself. Also, you will feel obligated to become better, because now someone is watching you. They are excited for your continued growth, and it will give them strength to attain new heights in their lives. Don't forget that.

Celebrate Your Wins

When I worked in the nonprofit organization, we had an exceptional way of recognizing those who were able to gain employment. Each time someone would come in and inform us that he or she landed a job, the entire staff would stop what they were doing, grab a small bell, and ring the bells of success throughout the office. Our clients usually beamed with pride because the bell was a symbol that they had earned their way to employment through diligent effort and faith. While you may not have a physical bell to celebrate your wins, there are other ways you can celebrate your success, no matter how big or small. I recommend creating "wins" jar, journal, folder, or wall. Whenever you reach a goal, make an accomplishment, or feel good about yourself, write down your victory. It is so easy to move through life quickly and forget about those moments that gave us the strength to move on and keep trying. Make celebrating your wins a regular part of life so that you stay motivated in your journey to freedom.

Conclusion

I've come a long way from that crazy 18-year-old girl with THUG LIFE tattooed on her chest. For a long time, I felt confined to a box. People told me exactly who they thought I would be and unfortunately, I didn't have the confidence to know I am the master of my destiny and capabilities. So, I opted to be basic, follow the crowd, and refuse my potential. Fortunately, there were people around me who didn't let me fall and pushed me to a better me. It didn't matter if I was young, black, skinny, "too smart" – none of those things matter when God has plans beyond what the eye can see. I've done a lot; good and bad, seen a lot, and sure have accomplished a lot by the age of 26. And I continue to push to do more, be better, and be a better person to benefit those around me. I still have a lot to learn, but I'm not slowing down, and I'm not stopping. I say all this to say, confidence is half of the journey to anywhere you want to be in your life. When you believe in yourself, your ideas, and your abilities, you place yourself on another level. Don't allow anyone to change your course or make you feel inadequate. You are enough. You are capable. And you are victorious. Believe that and claim it. In spite of everything that you have been through, you are still here.

The journey you have taken over time may have been difficult; yet, you found the courage and strength to persist anyway. Let that "yet" be enough to inspire you into a lifetime of abundance while you boldly exude and affirm confidence and freedom over your life.

Chapter Eight Reflection
1. Where are you in the freedom process?
2. Do you have an accountability partner? What would an idea accountability partner do for you?
3. How do you plan to celebrate your personal wins?
4. How can you allow "yet" to become a positive affirmation?

Afterword

Two years ago, I had the vision to write a book. Not just any old book, but a body of work that would add value to the world. During my time in graduate school, I hustled to collect facts, statistics, and data to support my thoughts around body image and self-esteem for black women. Growing up as a skinny black girl, I always wanted to "prove" that issues around those areas truly existed and was on a mission to do so through my blog and research.

As I began to work, I started to reflect on my own life and heard God tell me that this book required my story, no matter how painful, or traumatic I believed it was. Soon the book became much more than a guide to healthy "body image" because I realize those issues became a gateway to other crucial dilemmas women often place at the back of our minds to survive.

At first, I fought this revelation, often putting off the writing process to avoid reintroducing myself to parts of my past. When you come from painful, and sometimes self-inflicted situations, you desire to run away, both literally and figuratively. But as I continued to remove the bandages from my past, read emails and comments from women who have been impacted by my blog, skinnyblackgirlscode.com, I realized this book was much bigger than my fear of being judged. I needed to become transparent because there are women and girls, who have hurt as much as I have in my life. It would be selfish not to share how I've turned my turmoil into a testimony of peace, freedom, and happiness.

As I shared the good, bad, and ugly moments of my life, I genuinely hope that my transparency helped you realize that freedom lies within forgiveness and the courage to be the best version of yourself no matter what life throws at you. There is so much of life ahead of you, but it takes a strong woman to recognize how she will resolve things that are holding her back from her greatest potential.

I'm far from a success story. I am a work-in-progress that is unbothered to admit that I have good days and bad days. Freedom is not a permanent concept; it requires an ongoing effort to fight for the values and non-negotiables you define and implement in your life, regardless of what stage in life you set them.

Self-awareness is your secret weapon to battling for freedom. As long as you decompartmentalize your emotions, communicate, be solid in your faith, allow your purpose to manifest organically, surround yourself with friends, family, and partner who complement your growth, you unquestionably remain a contender of freely living a life by your own terms and defining your destiny.

About the Author

After being teased about being a "skinny black girl" from the blacktops of the playground to her first "grown-up" role in her career, Whitney Barkley decided to take her four-eyes and slim behind to the World Wide Web to express herself. In October 2014, the Skinny Black Girl's Code was born to help women overcome obstacles imposed by self-doubt, low self-esteem, and societal constructs to pursue a lifestyle that demands confidence and freedom.

Visit www.skinnyblackgirlscode.com to learn more about Whitney.